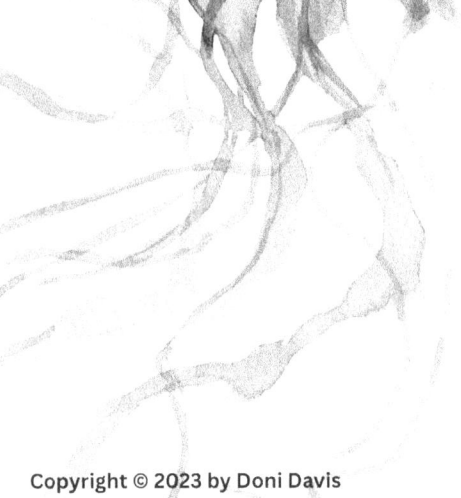

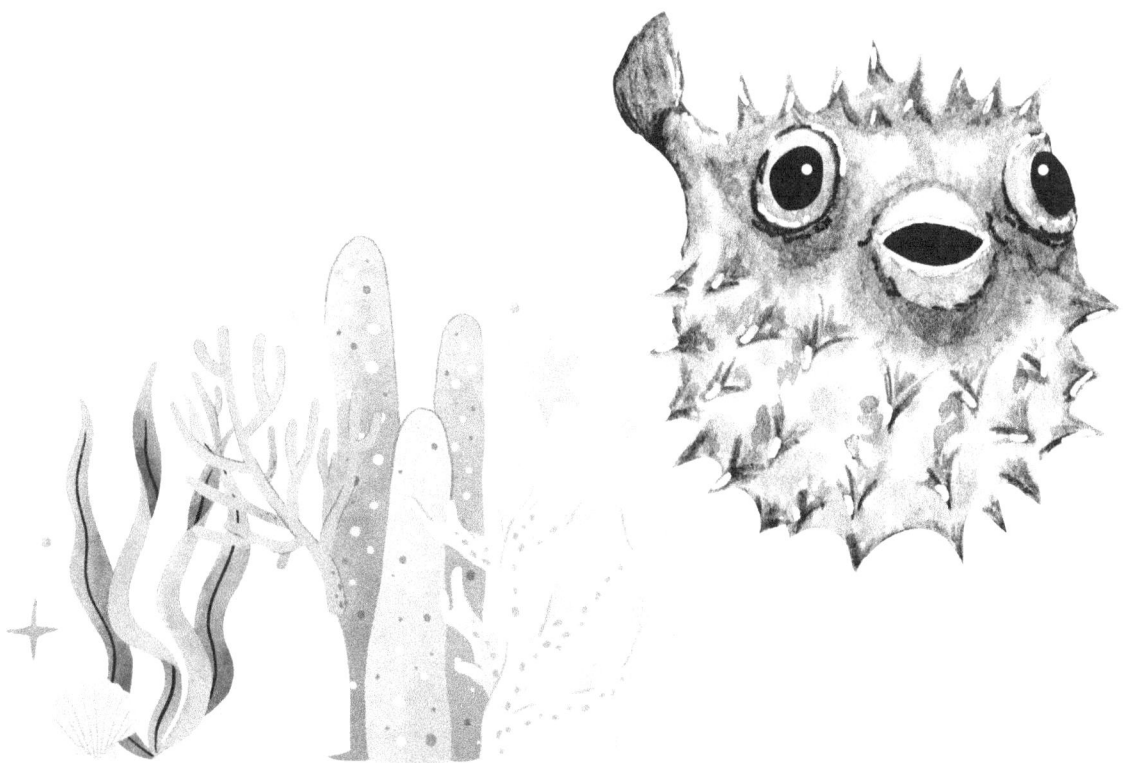

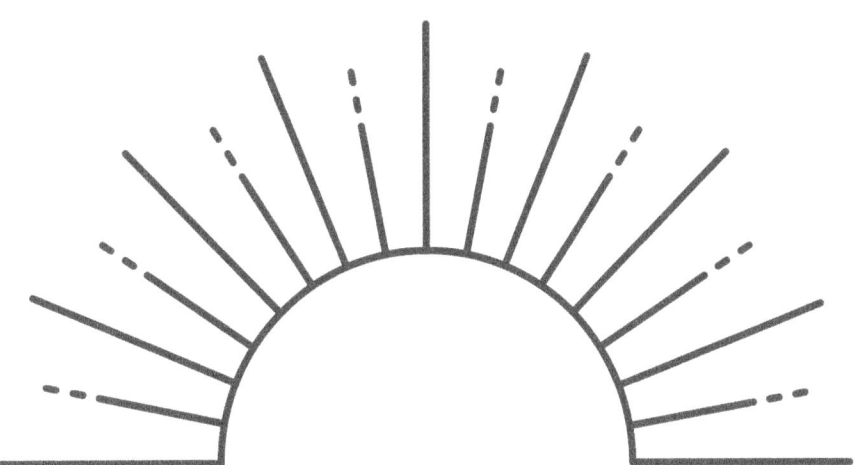

This book belongs to:

_____

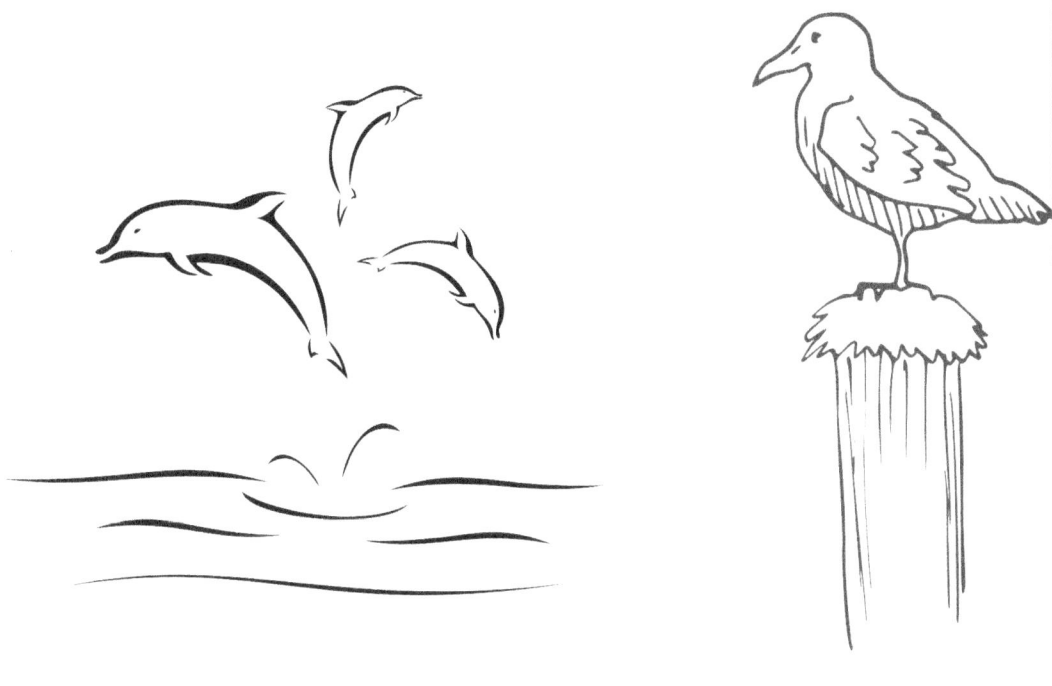

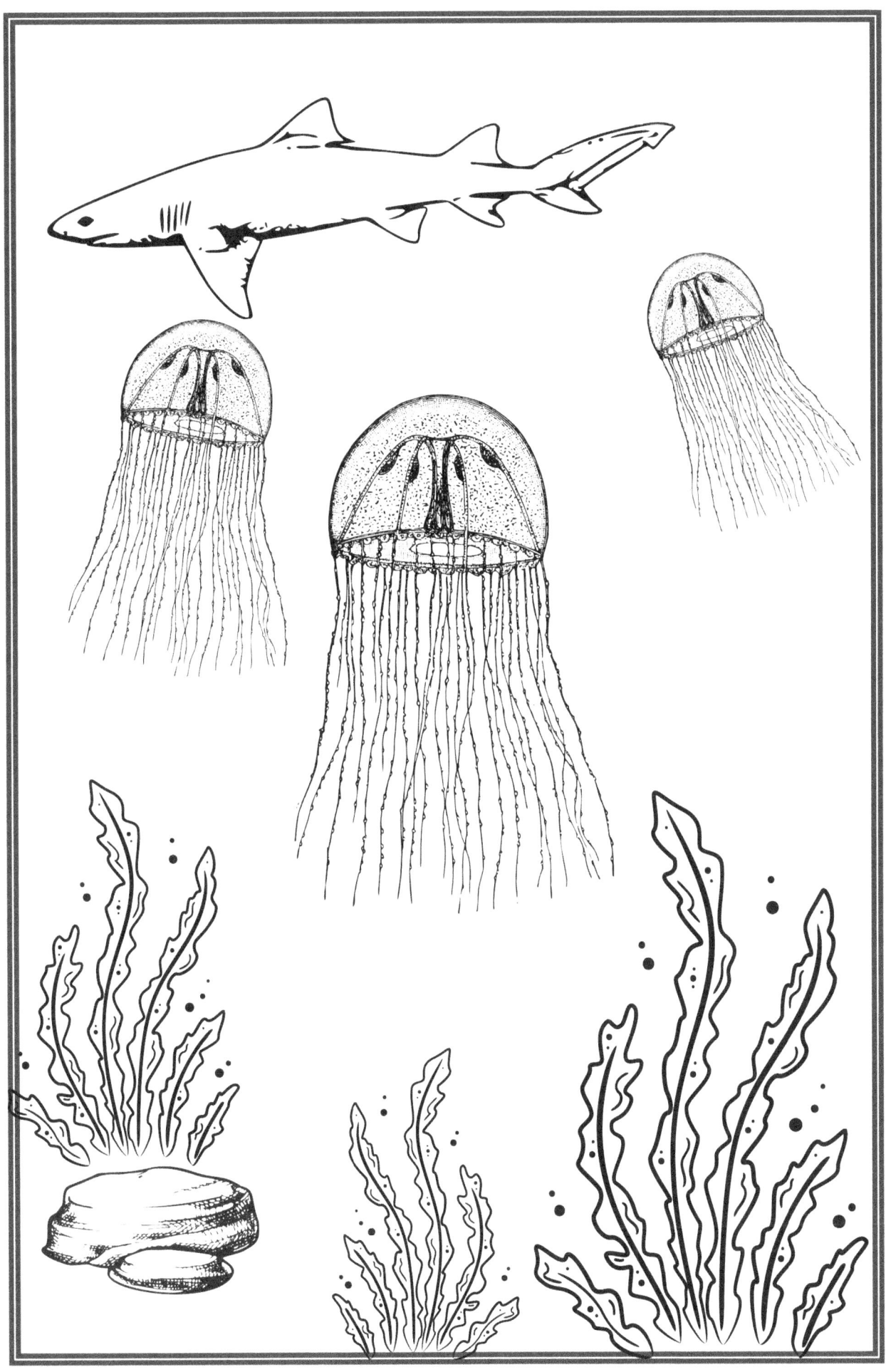

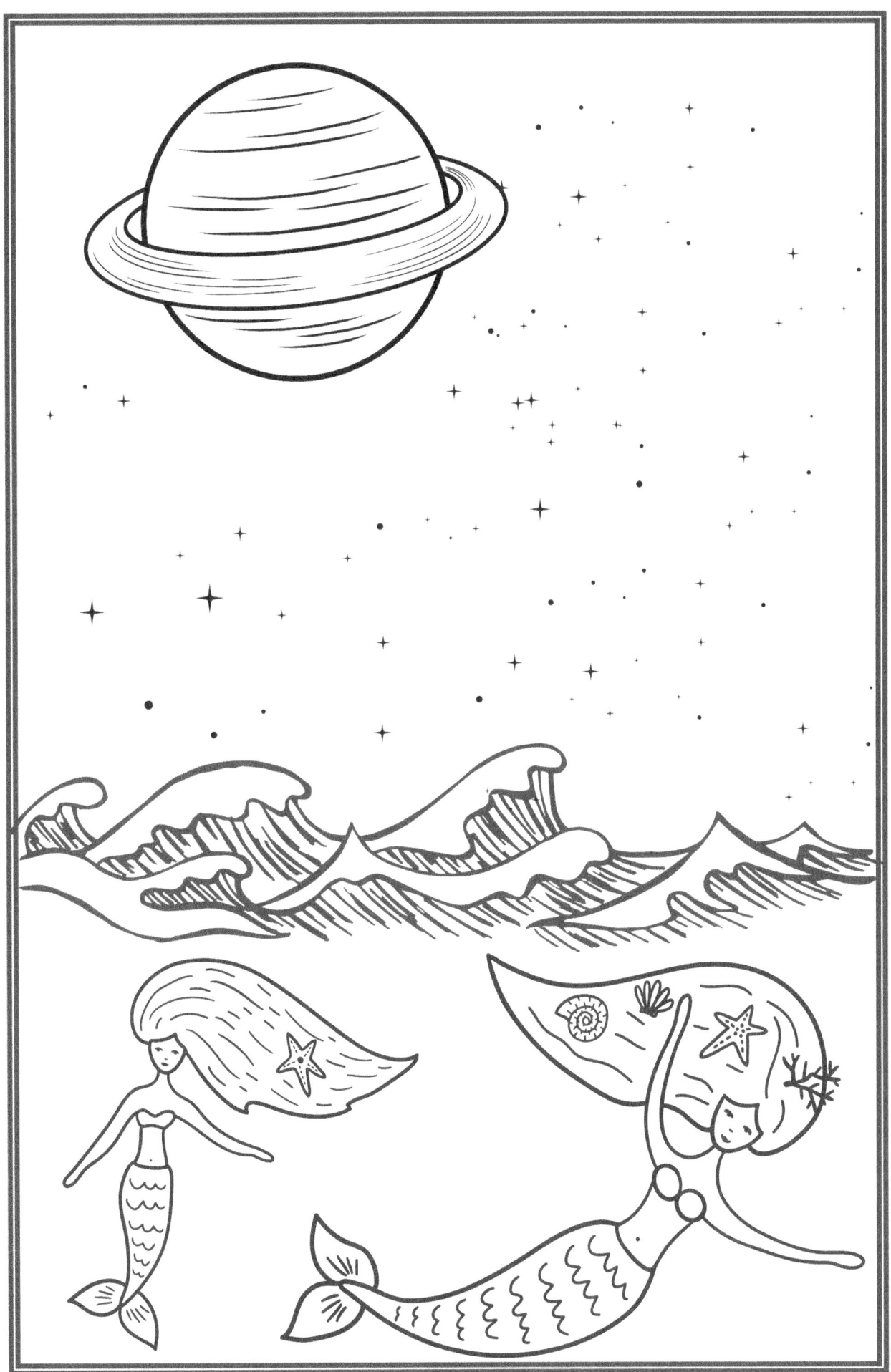

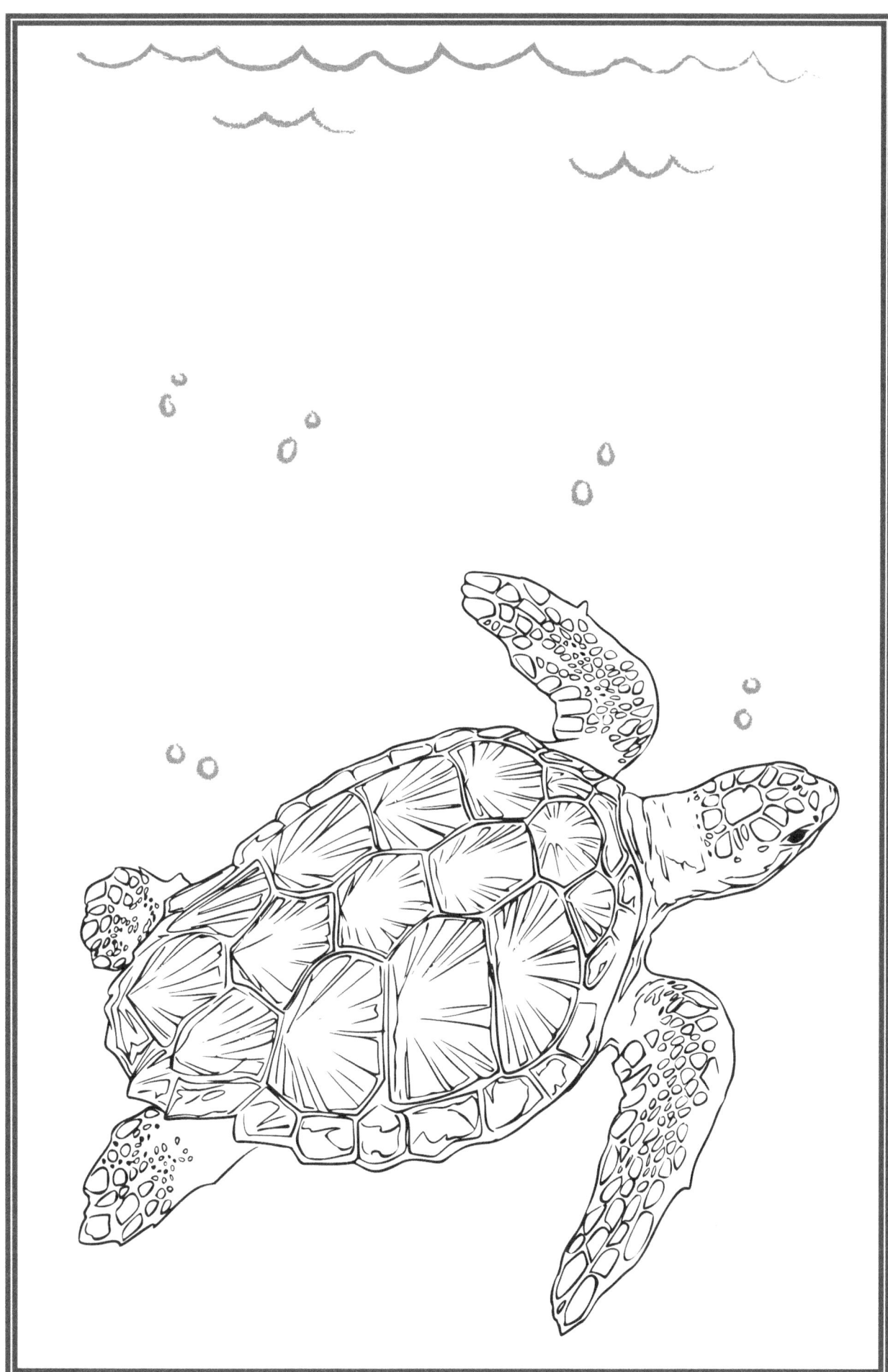

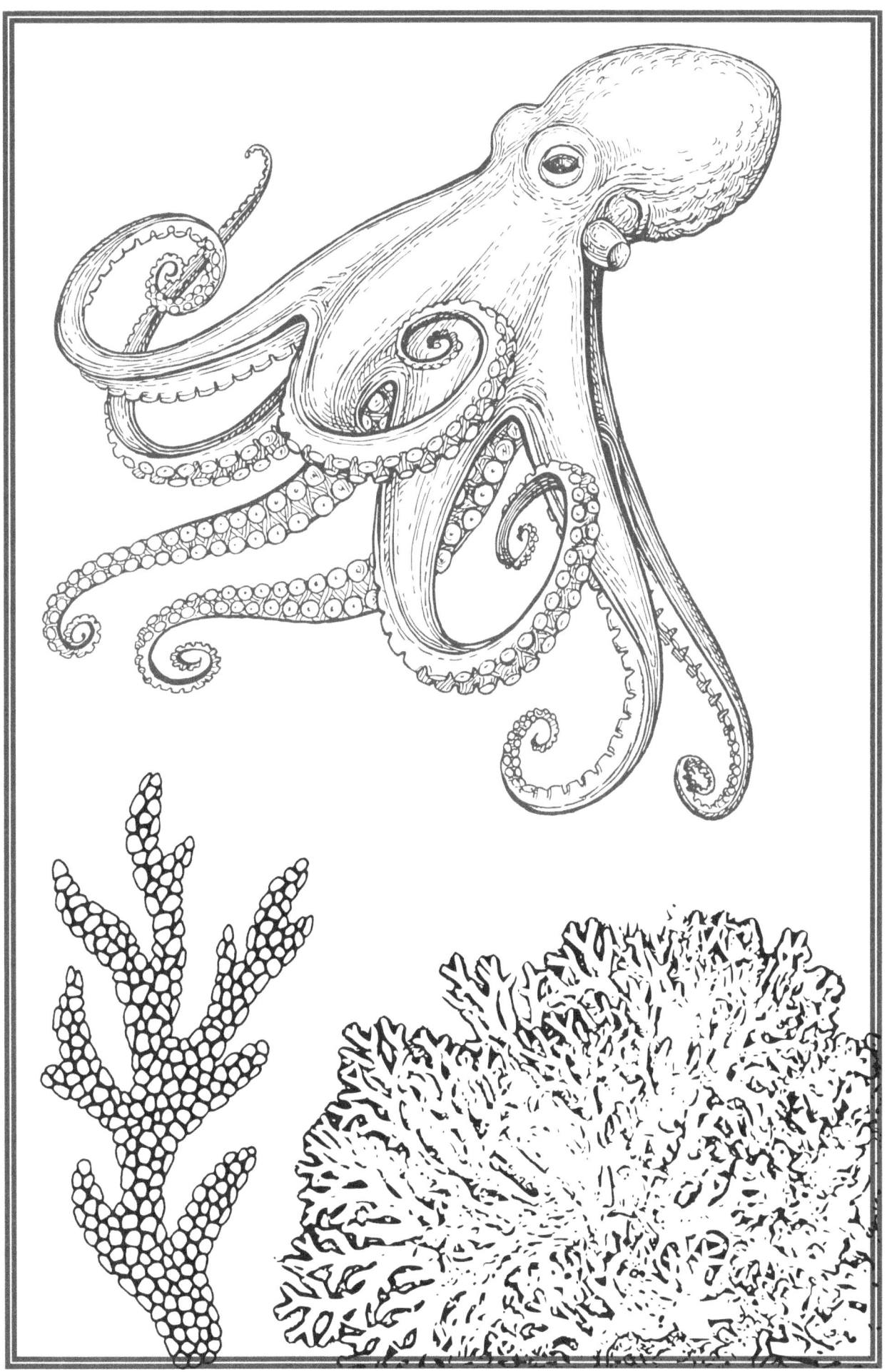

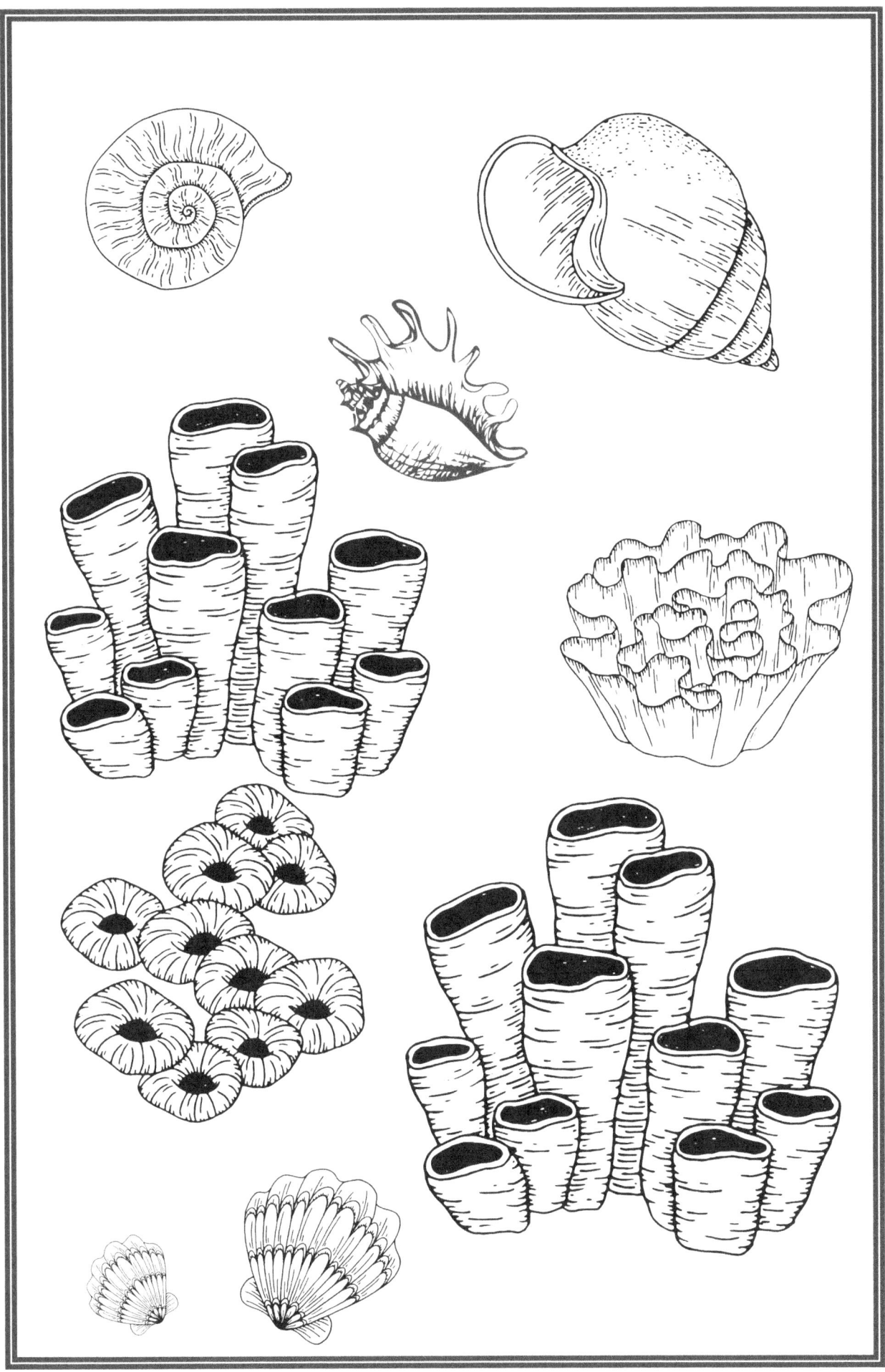

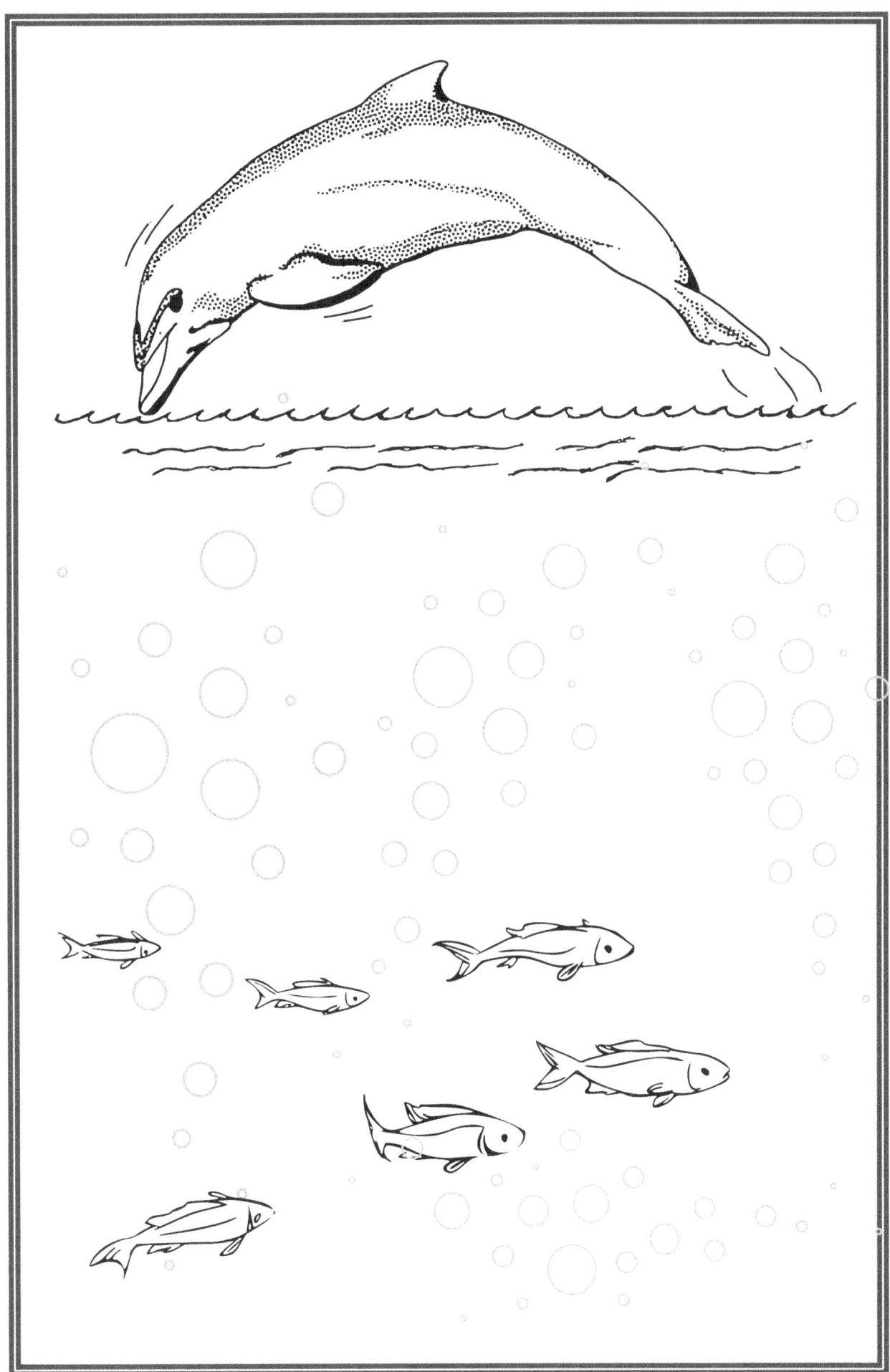

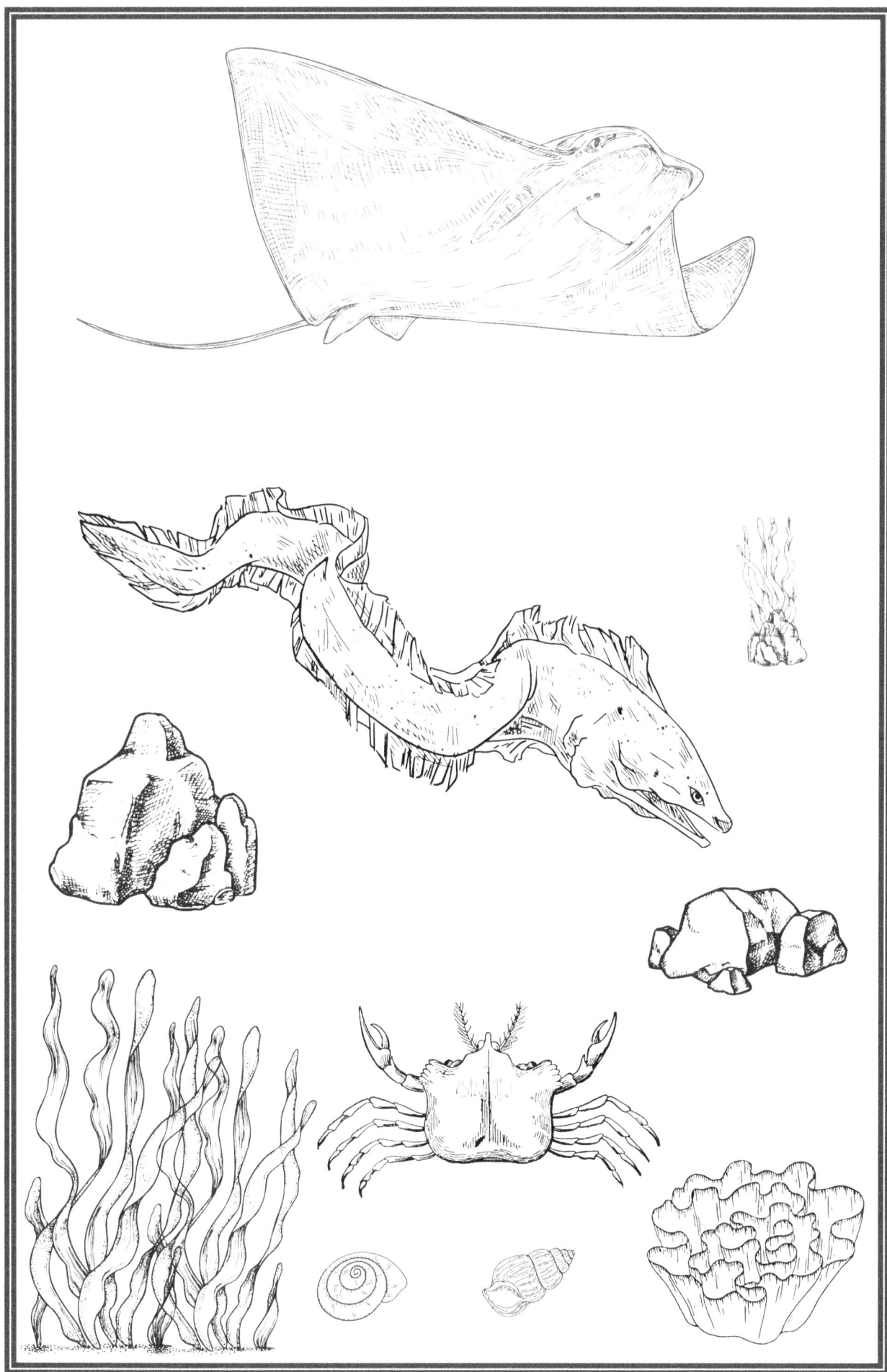

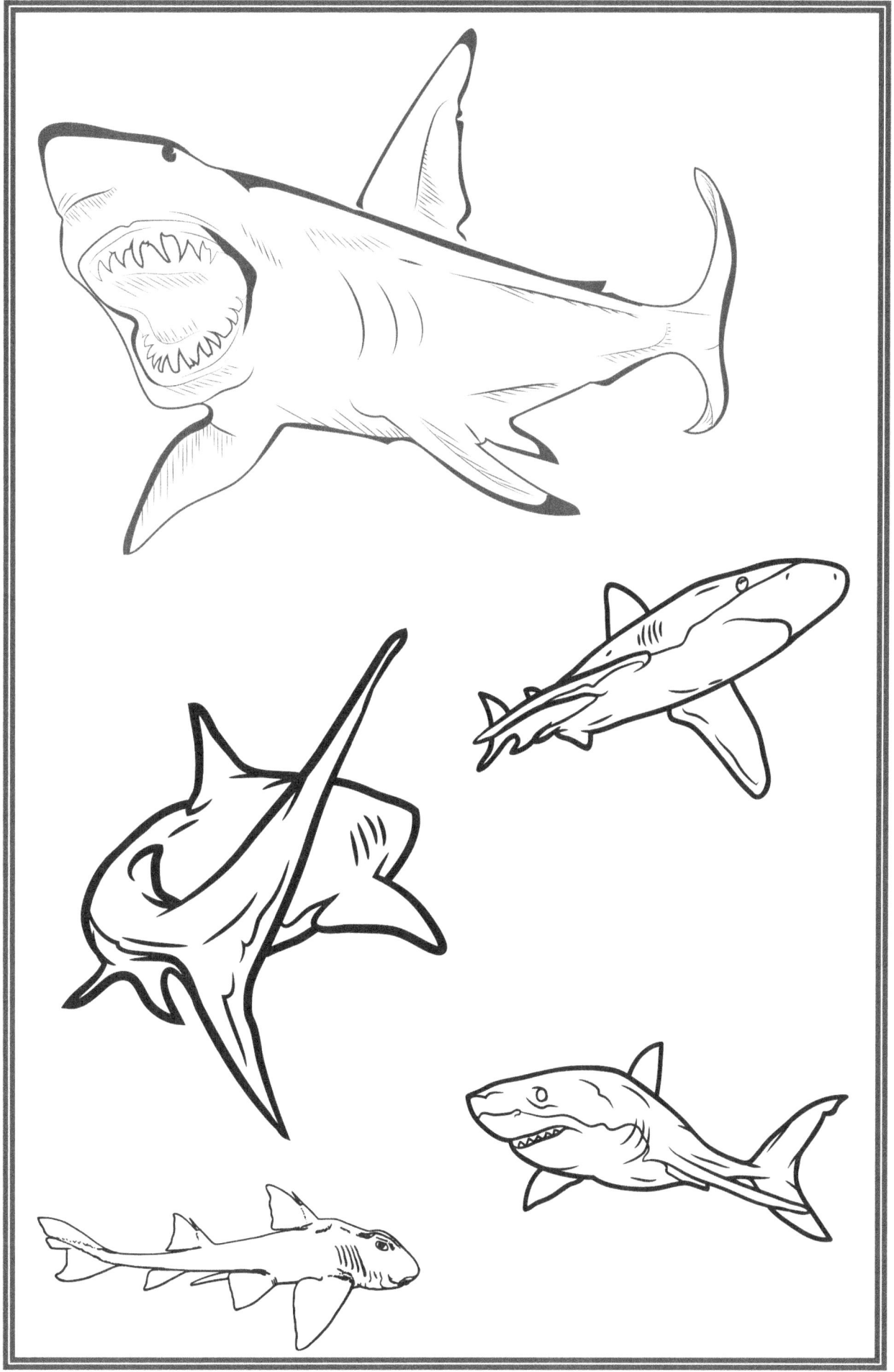

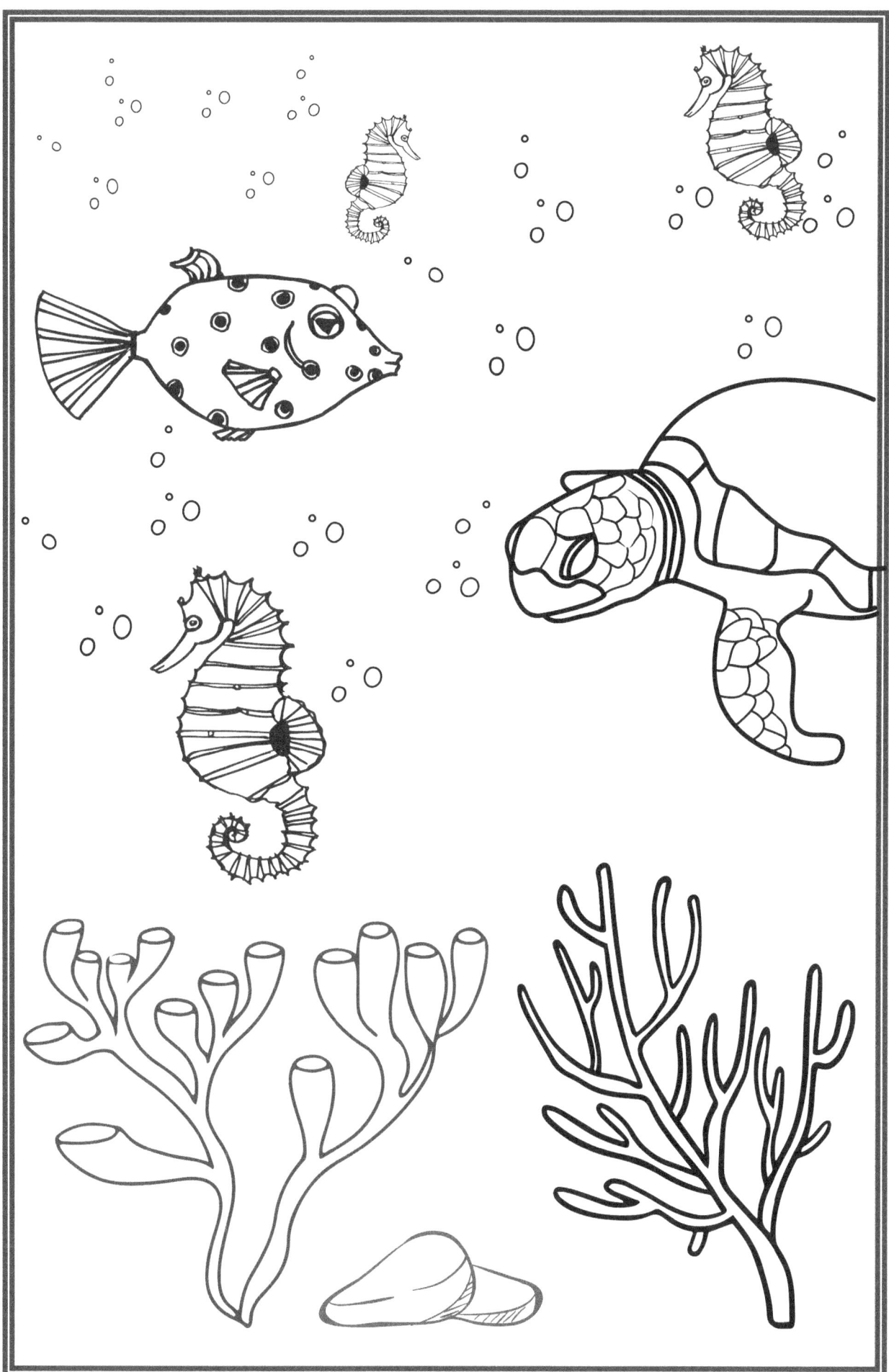

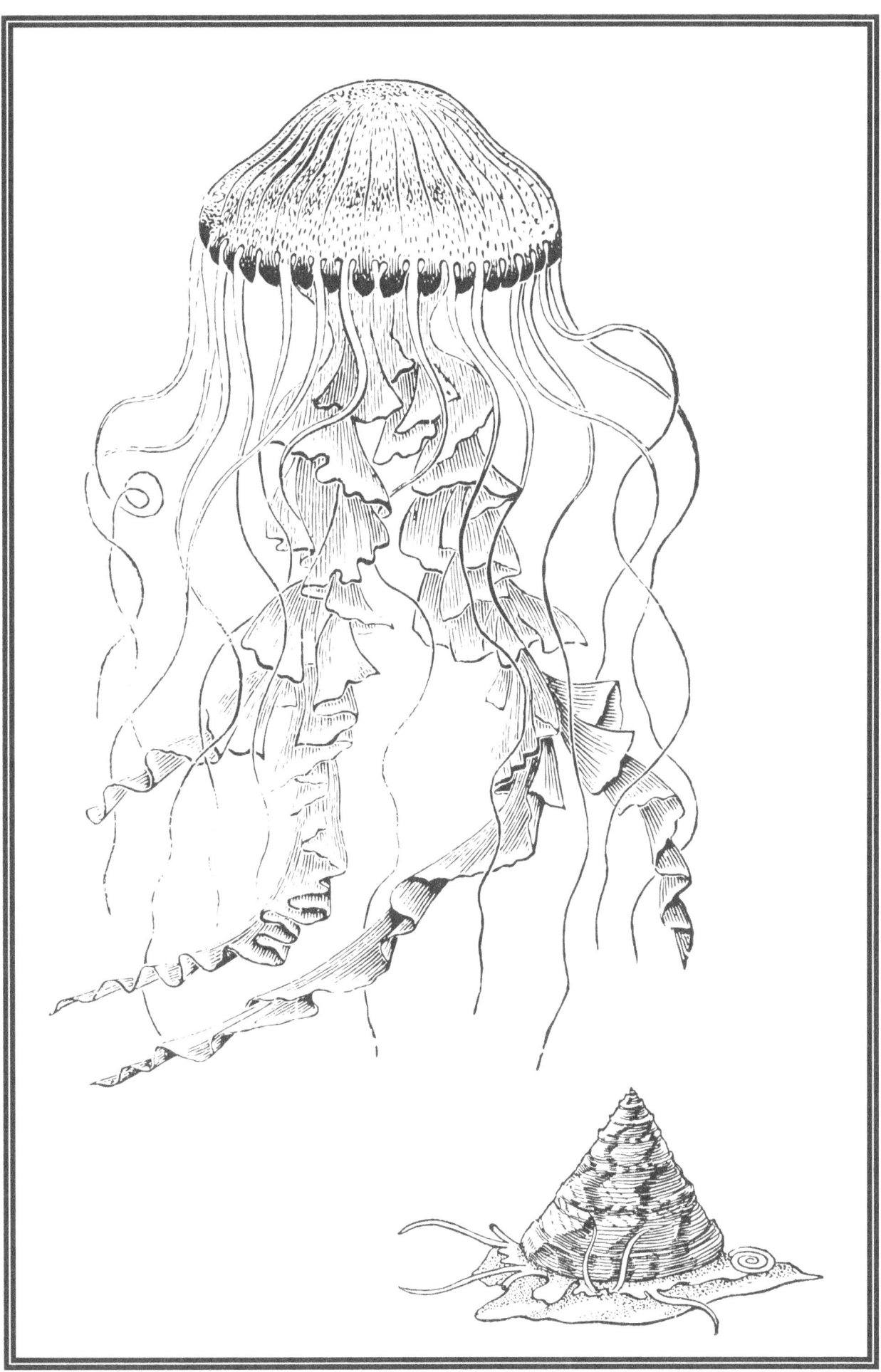

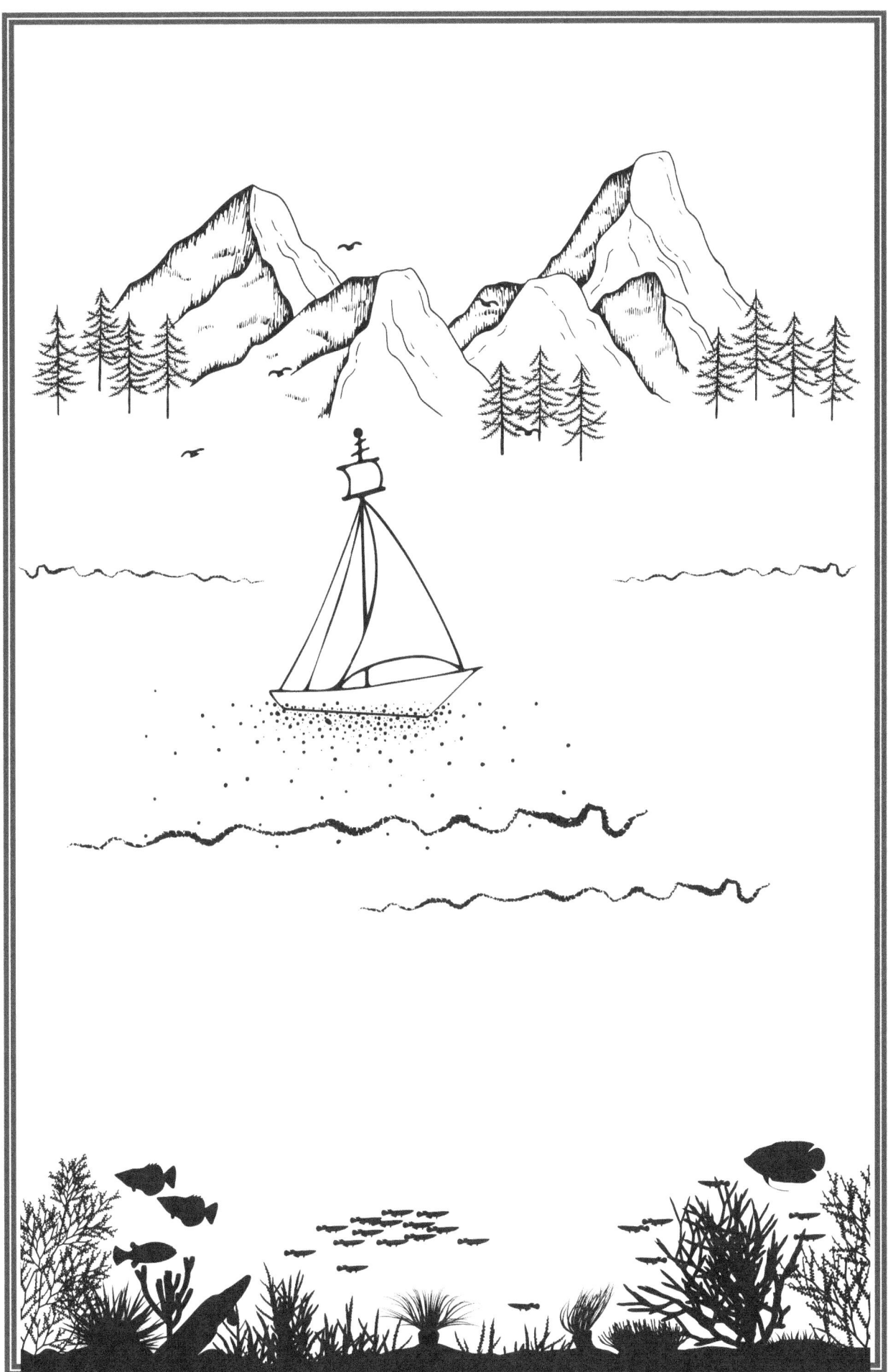

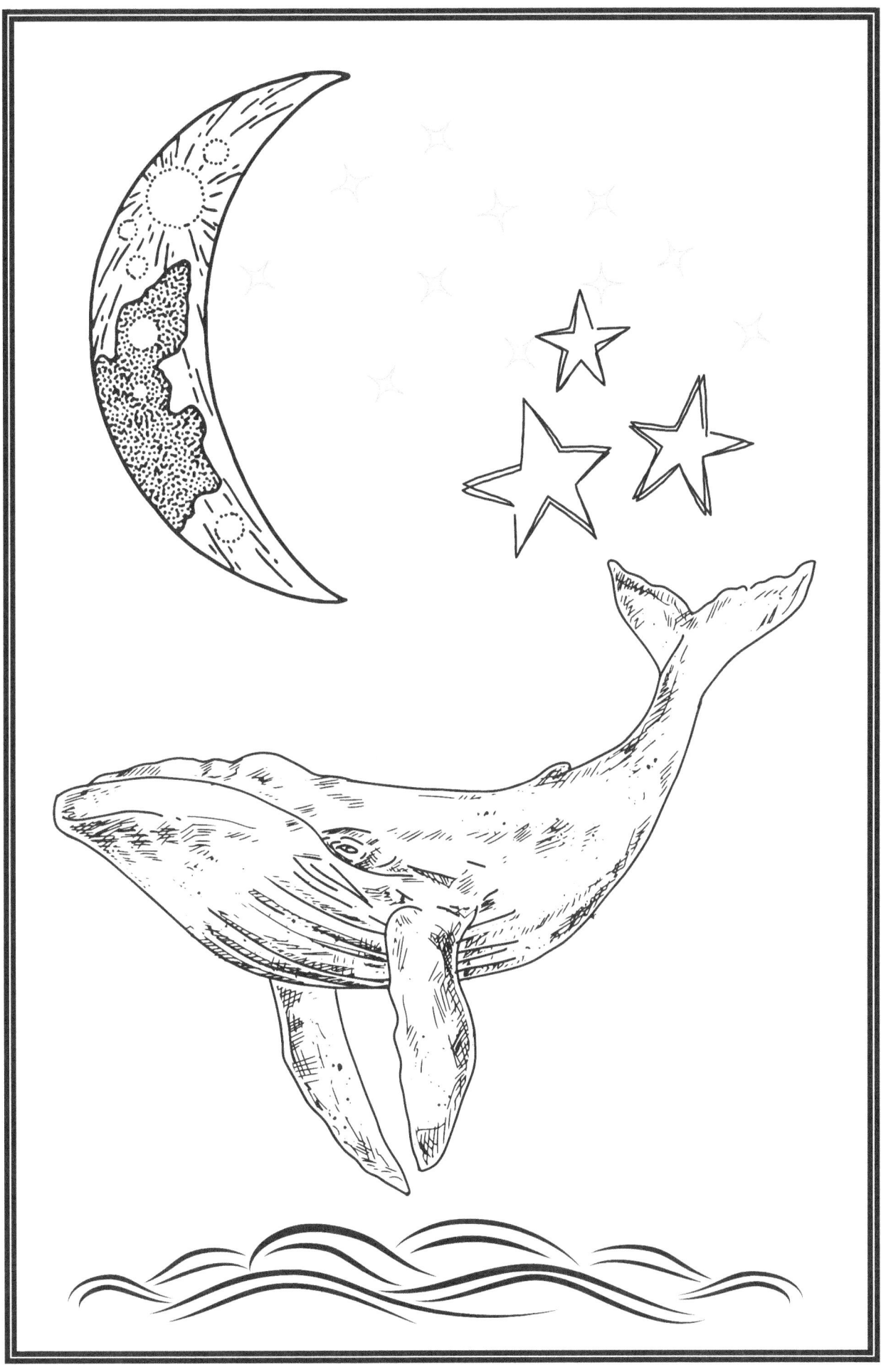

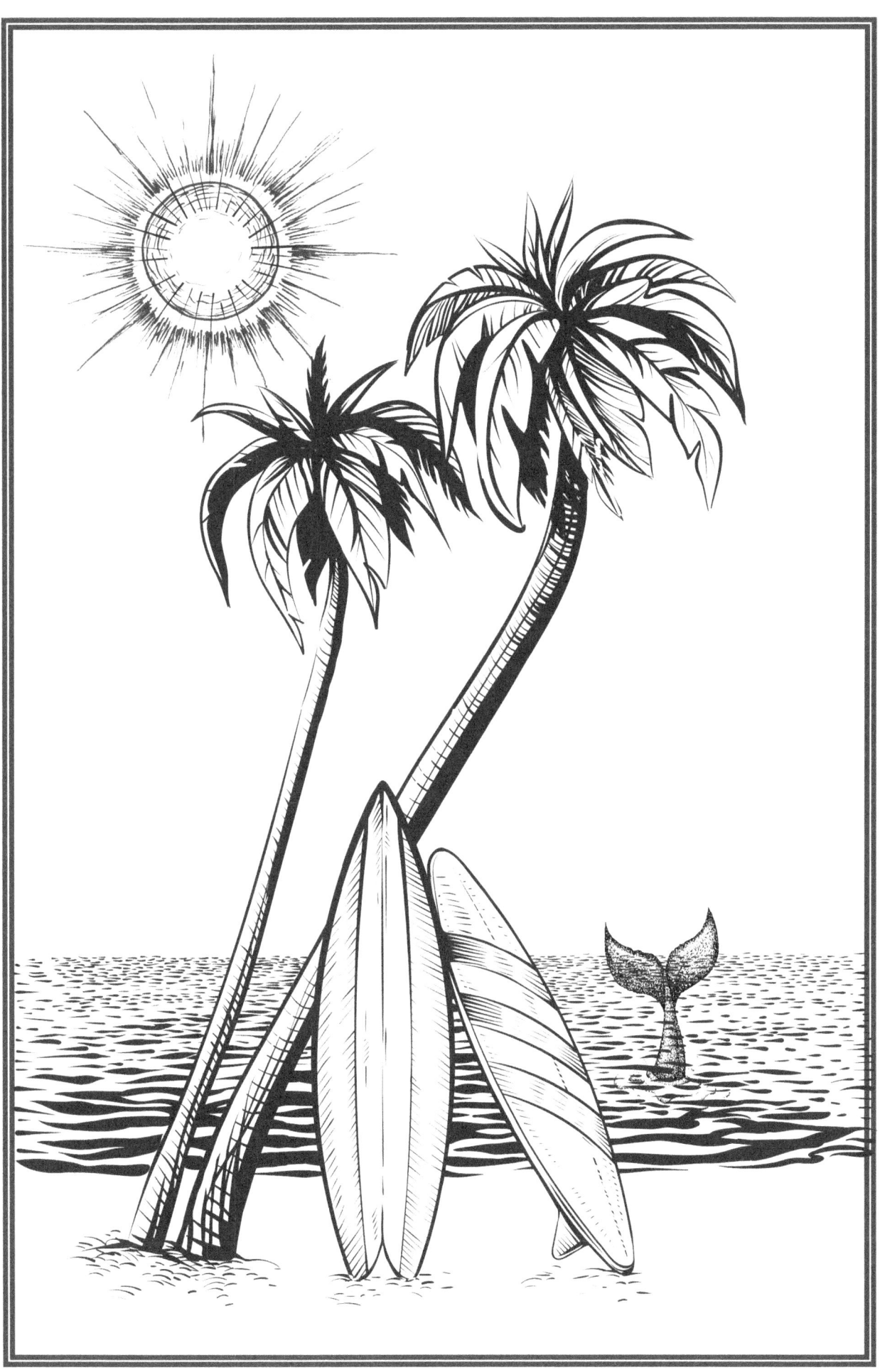

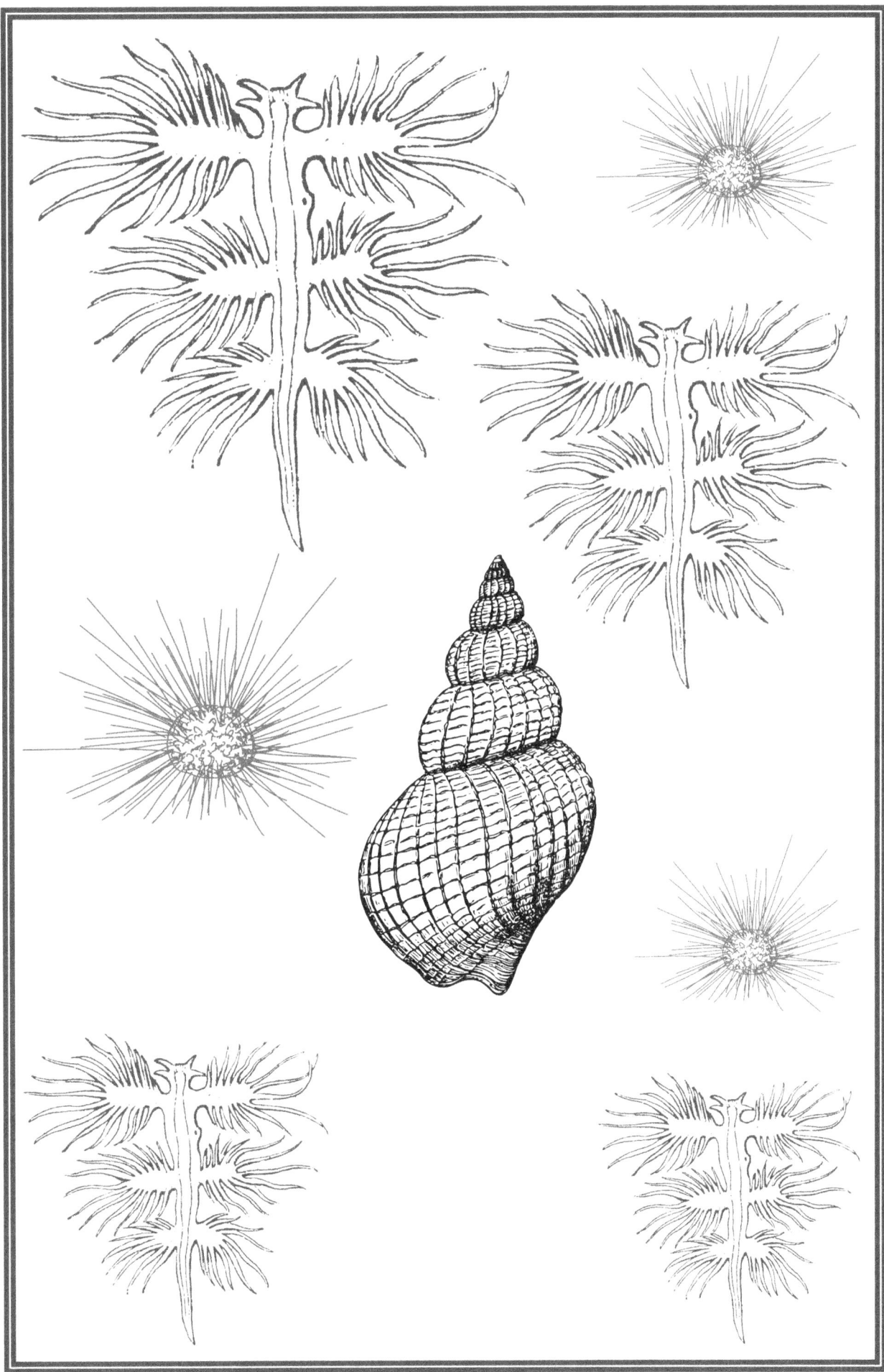

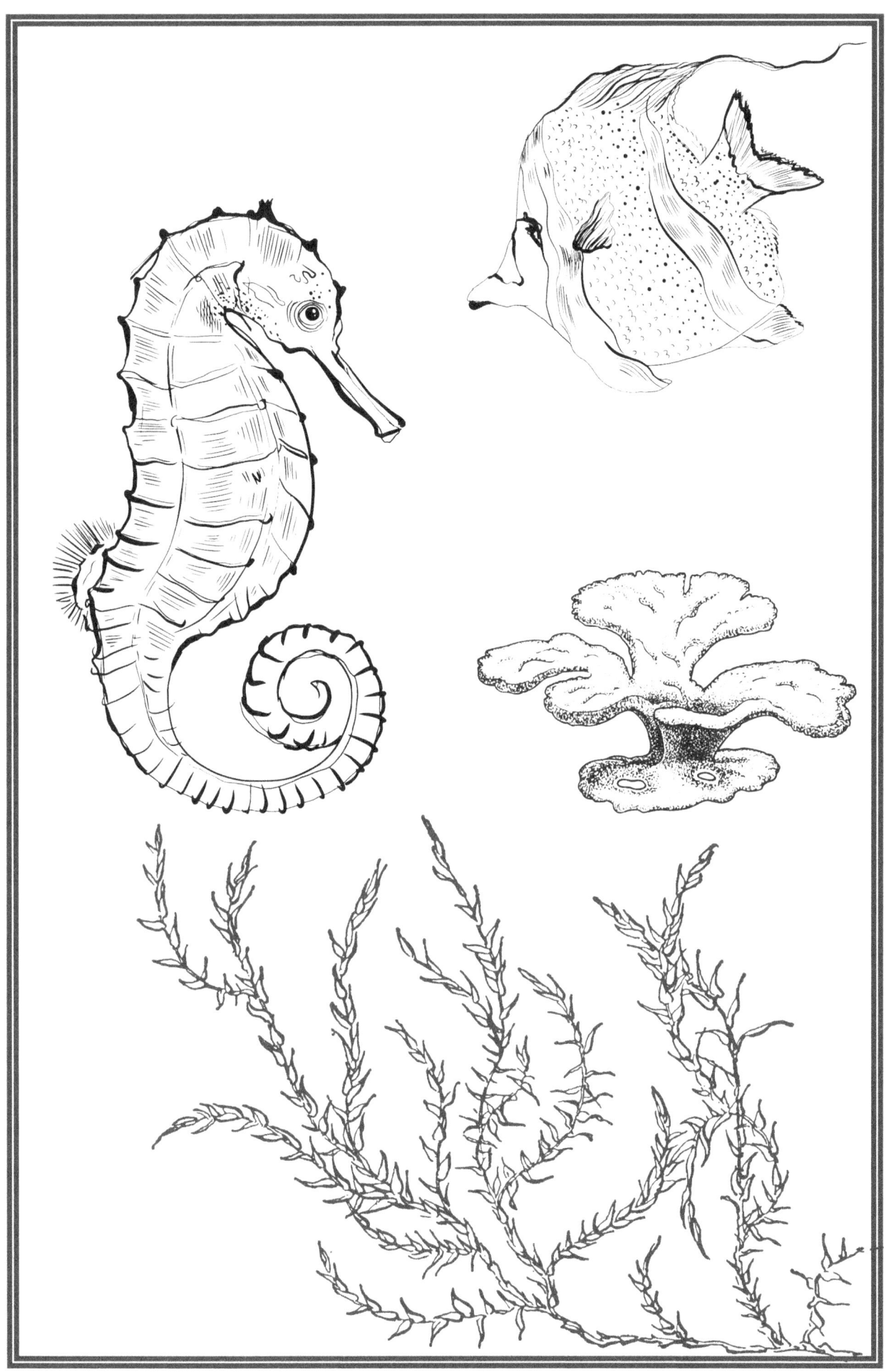

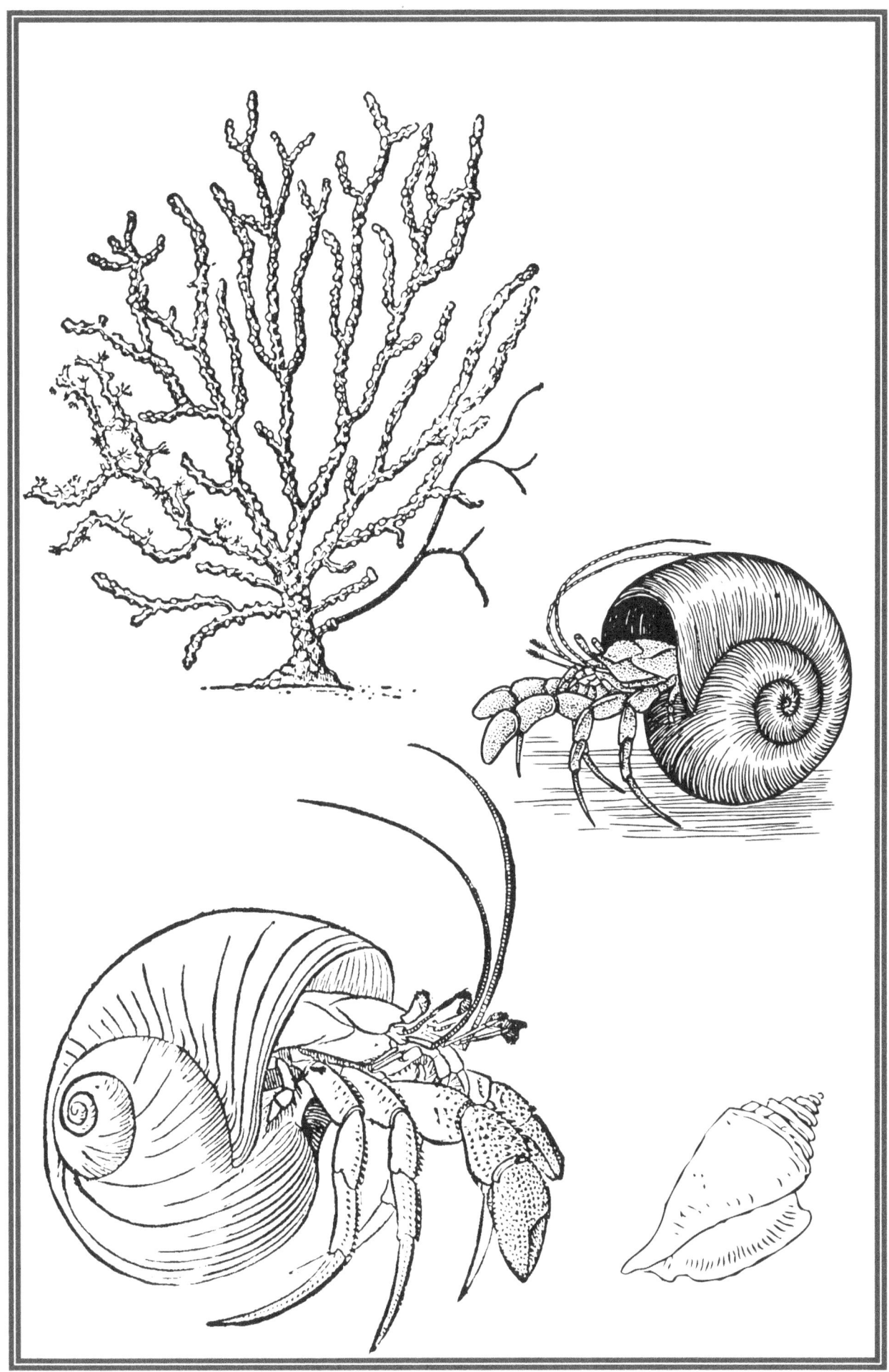

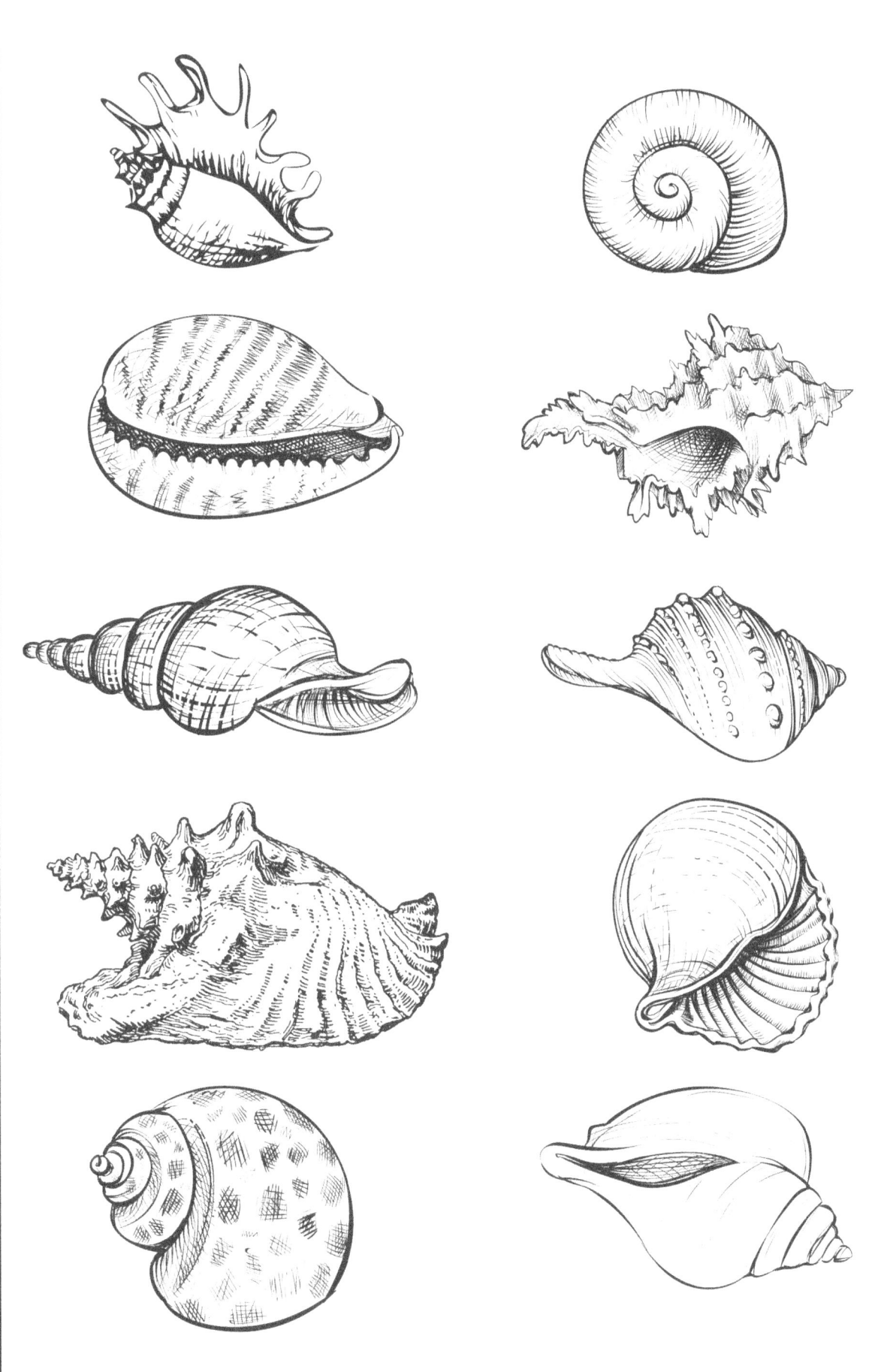

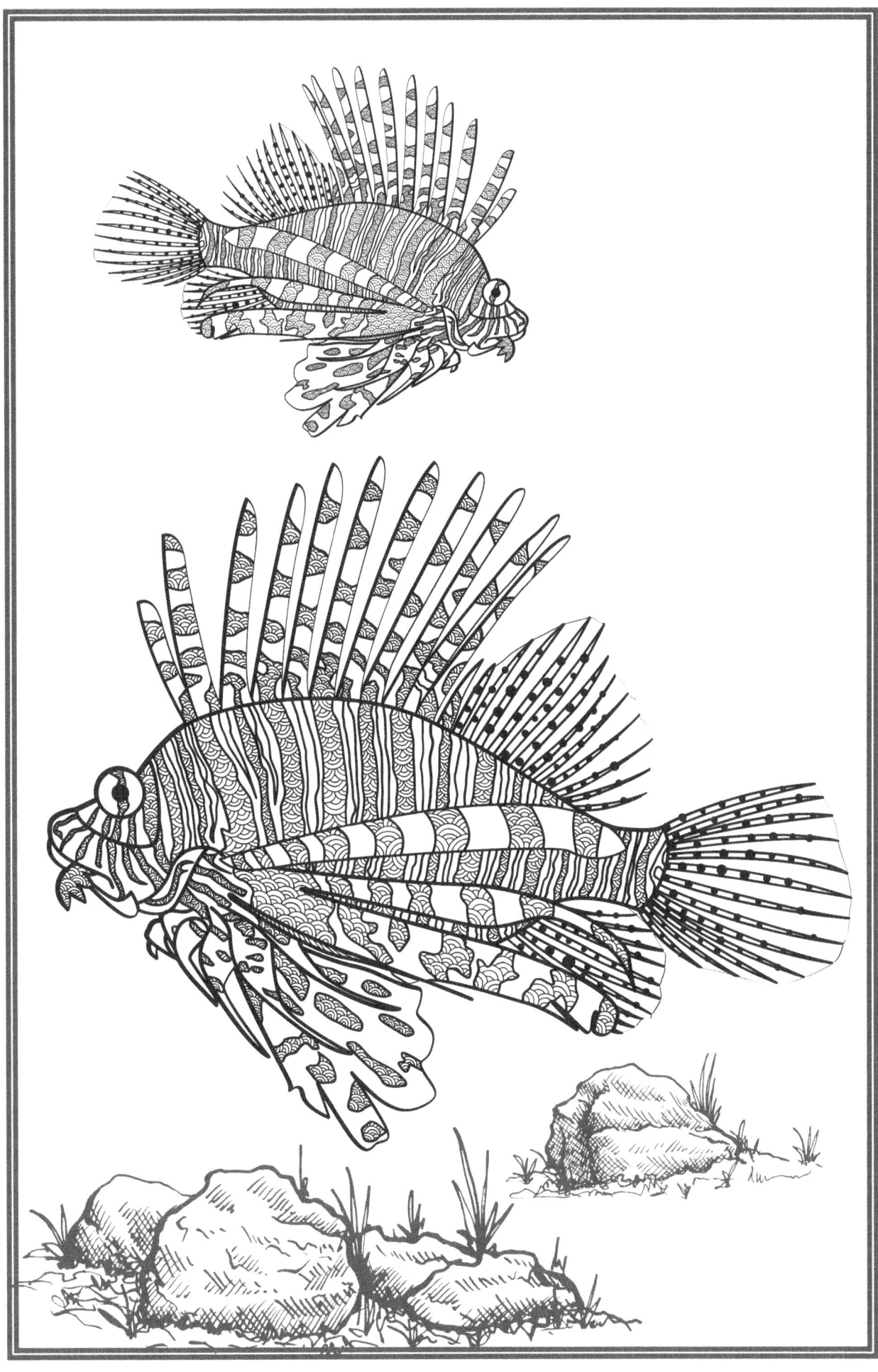

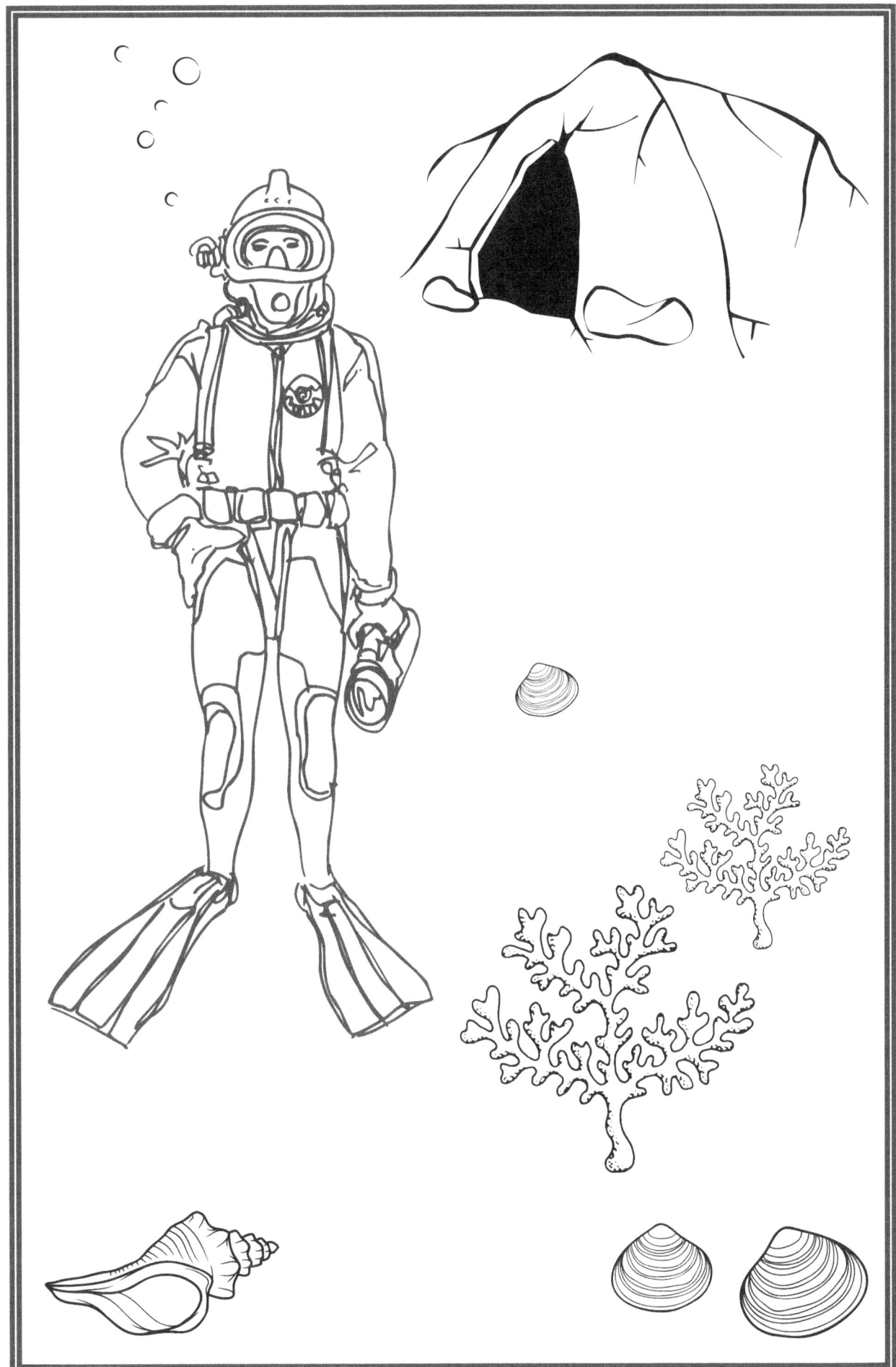

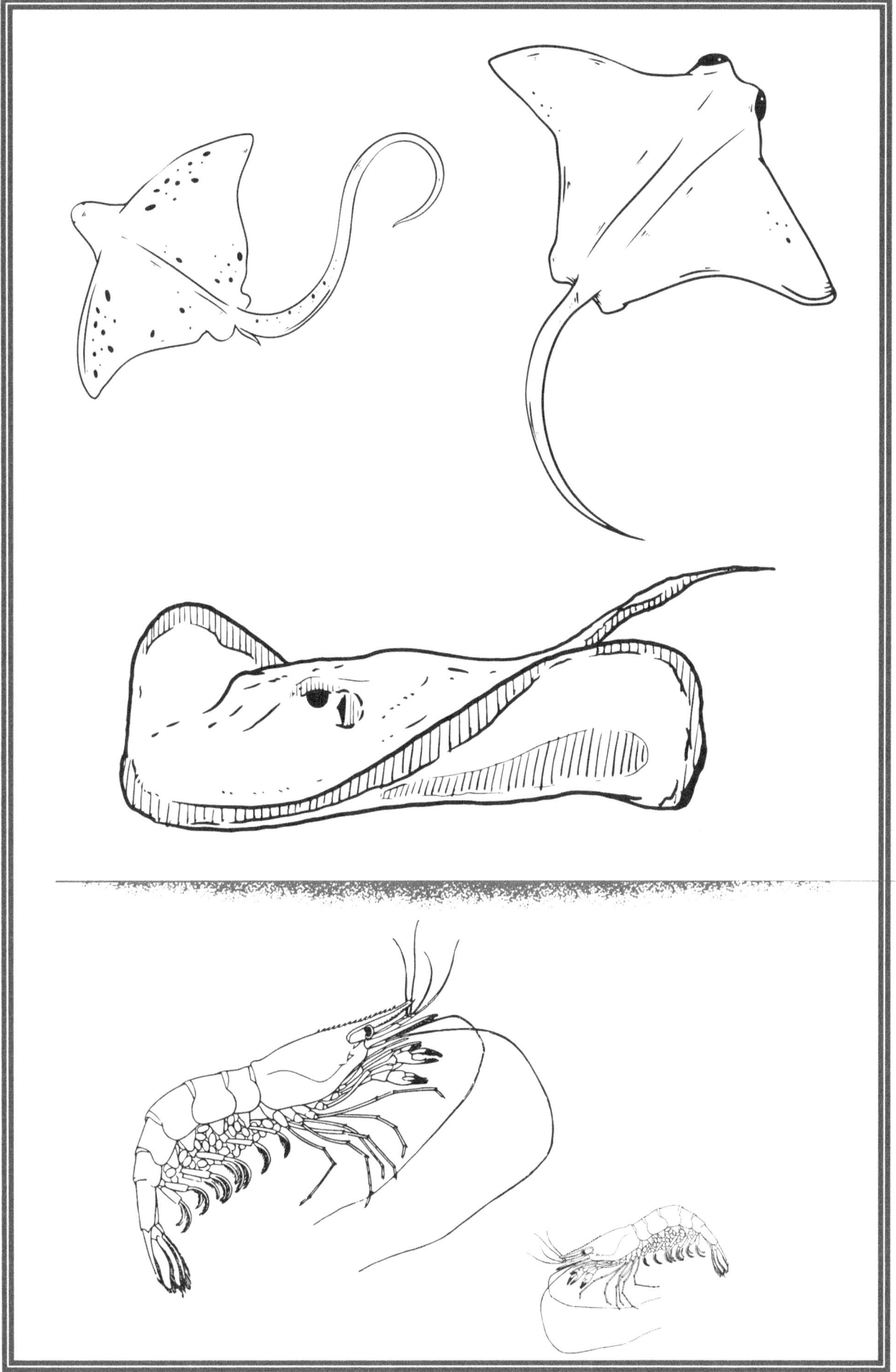

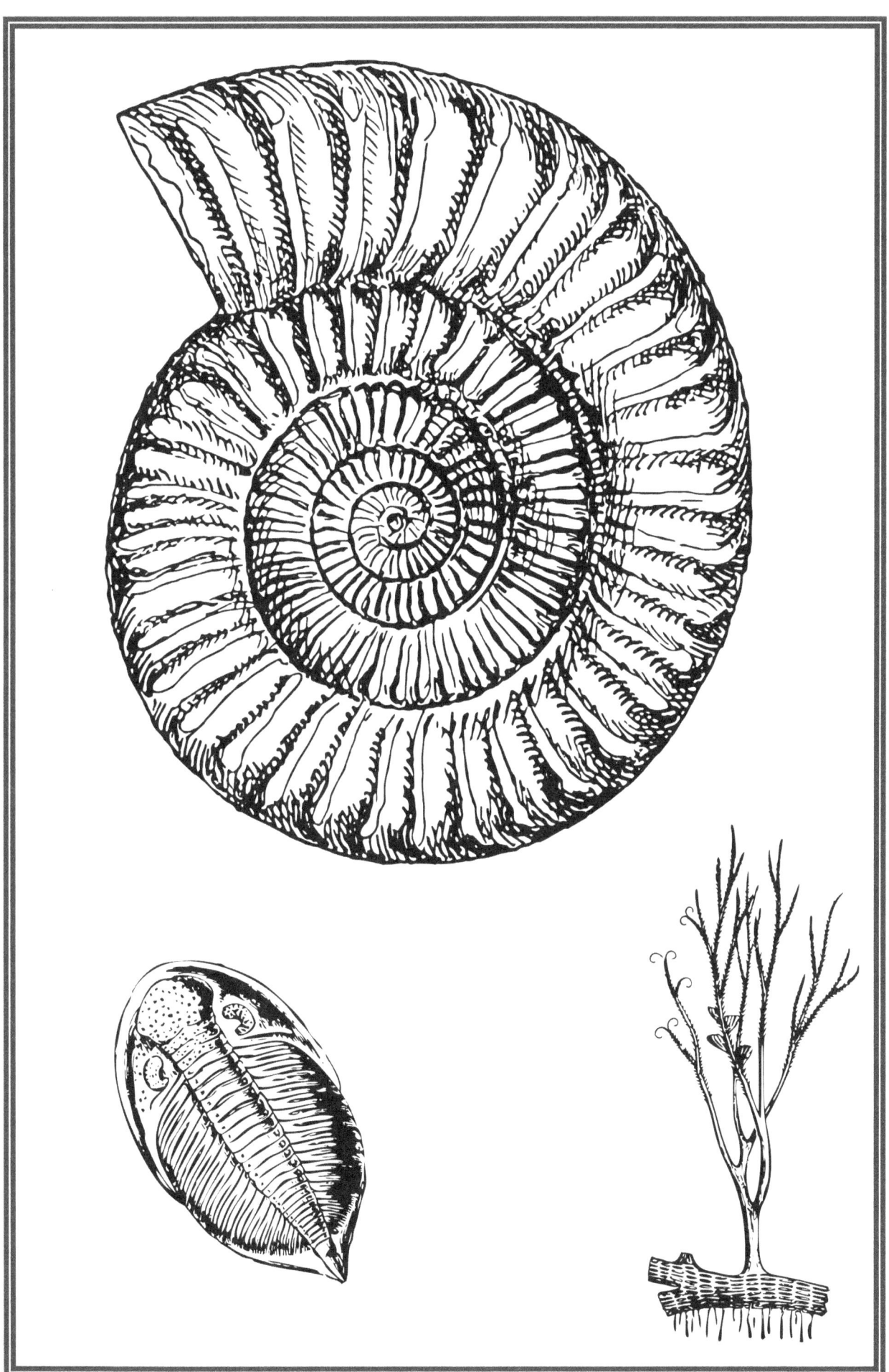

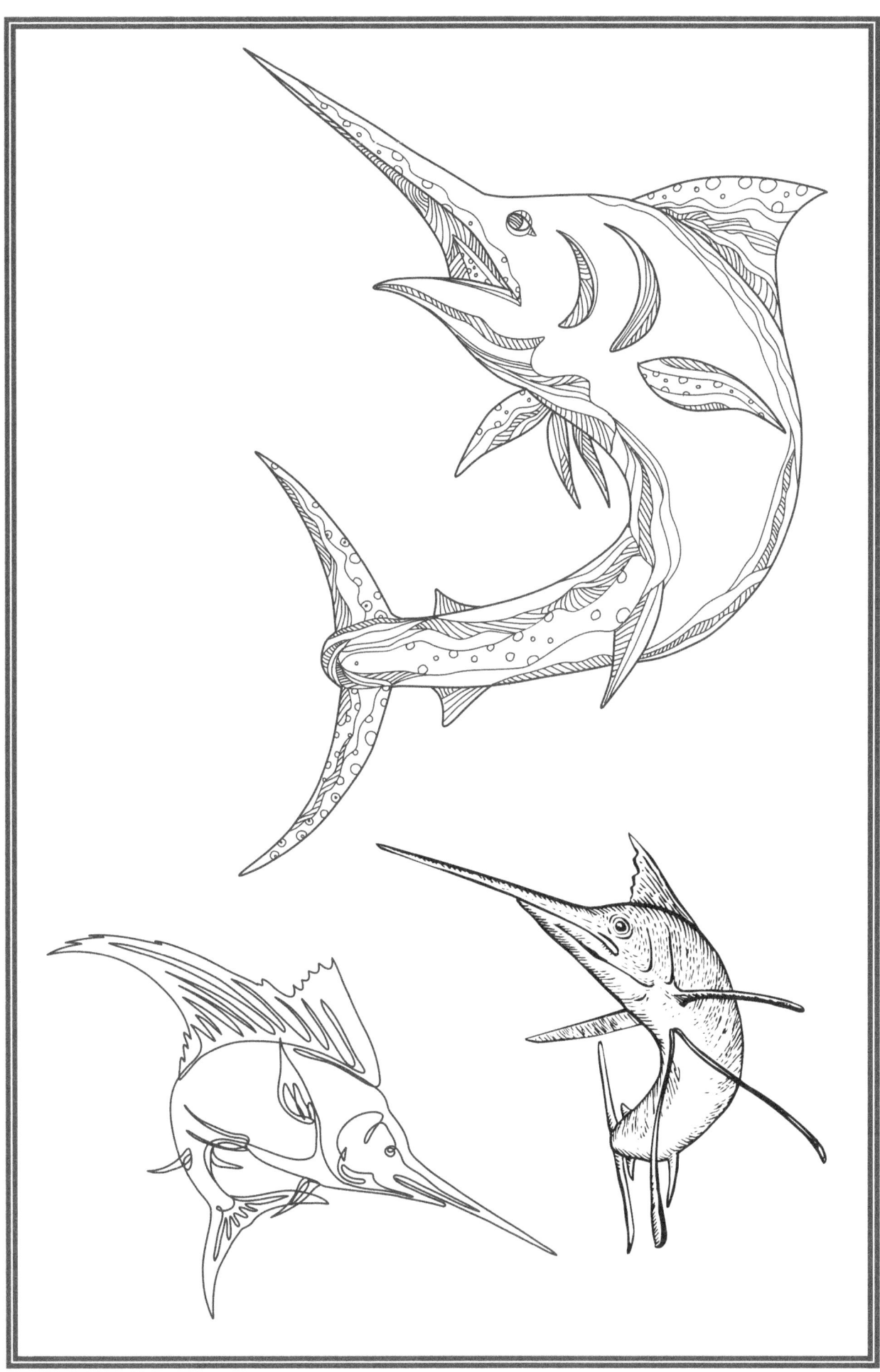

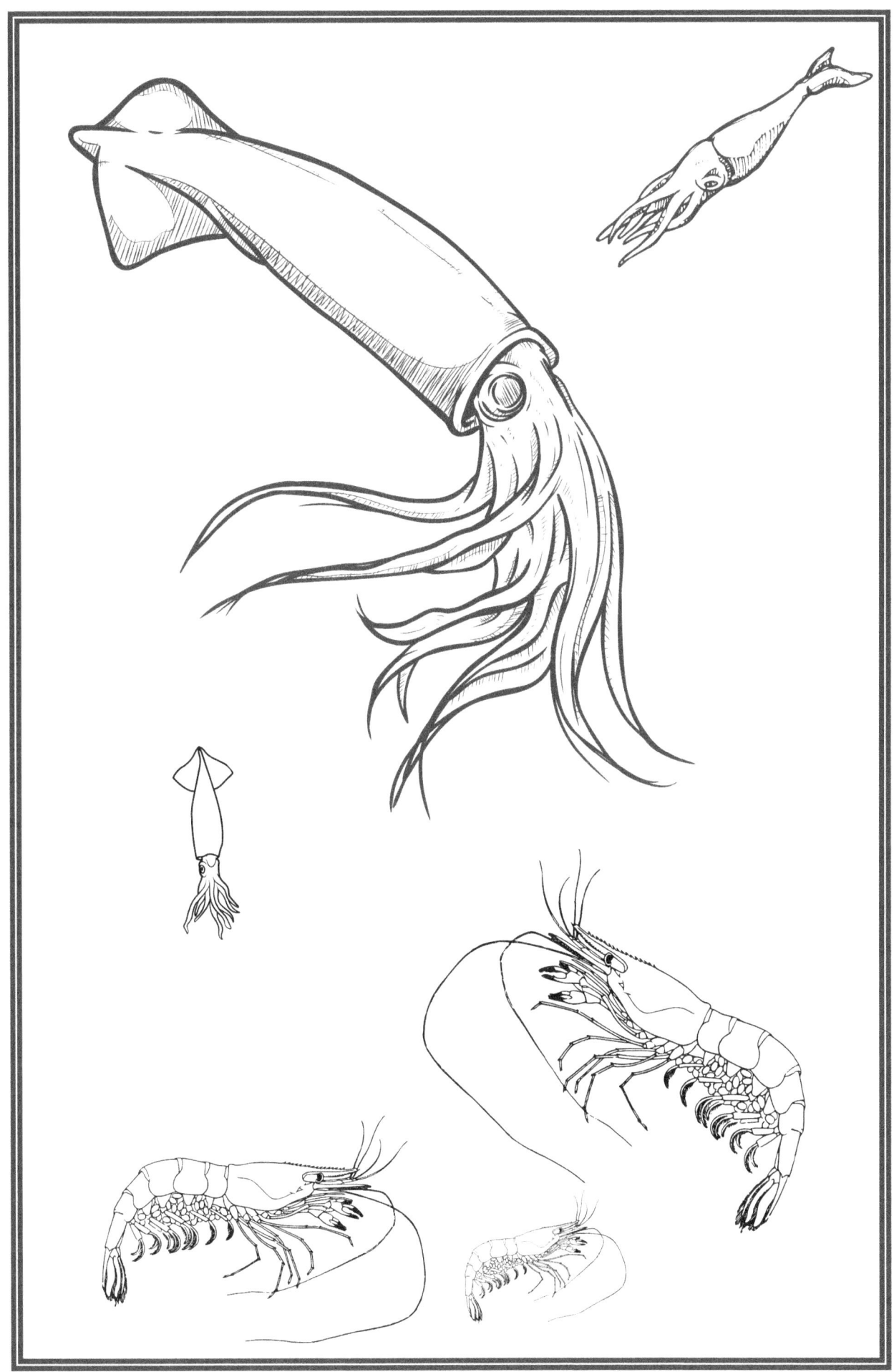

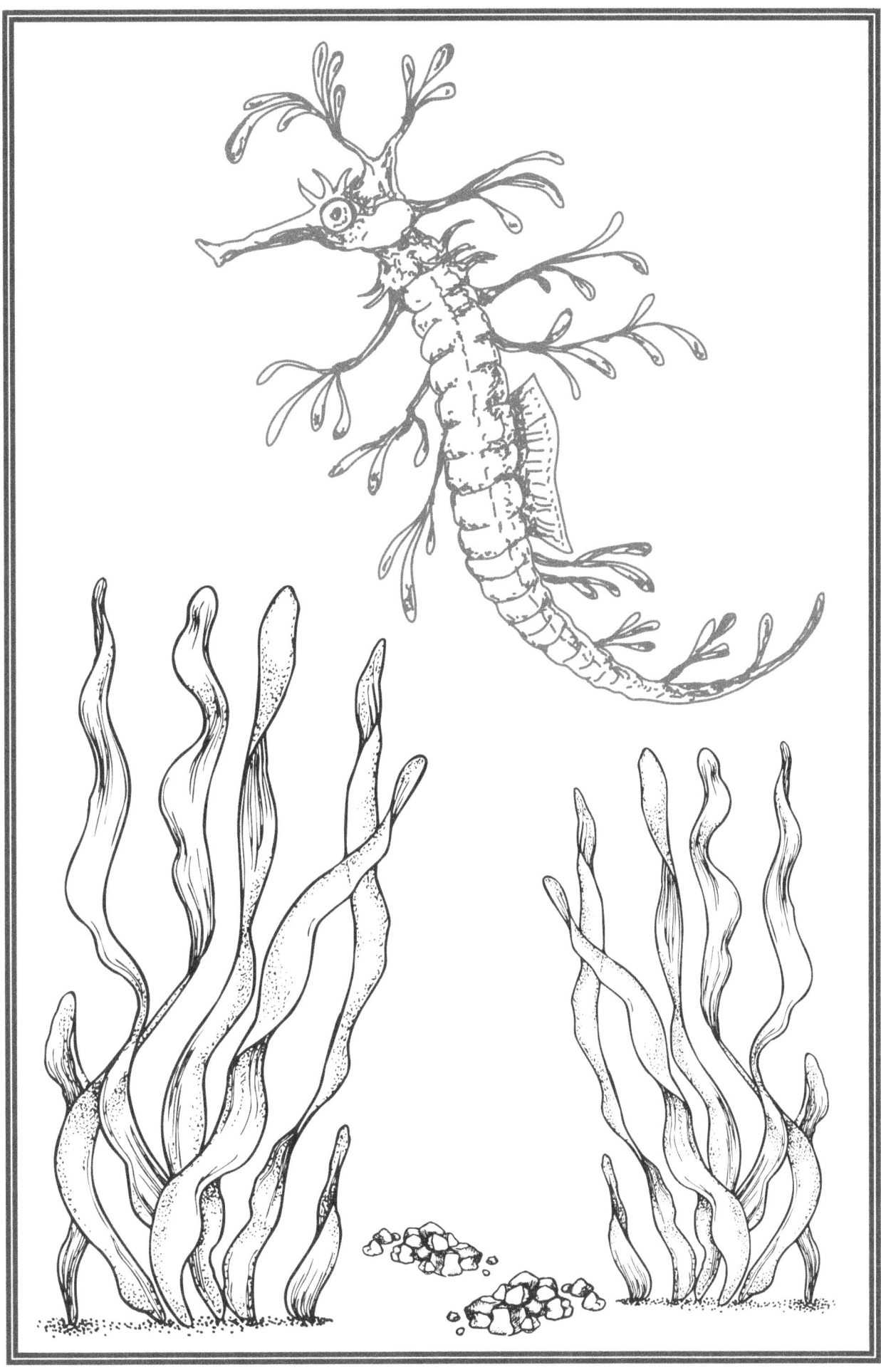

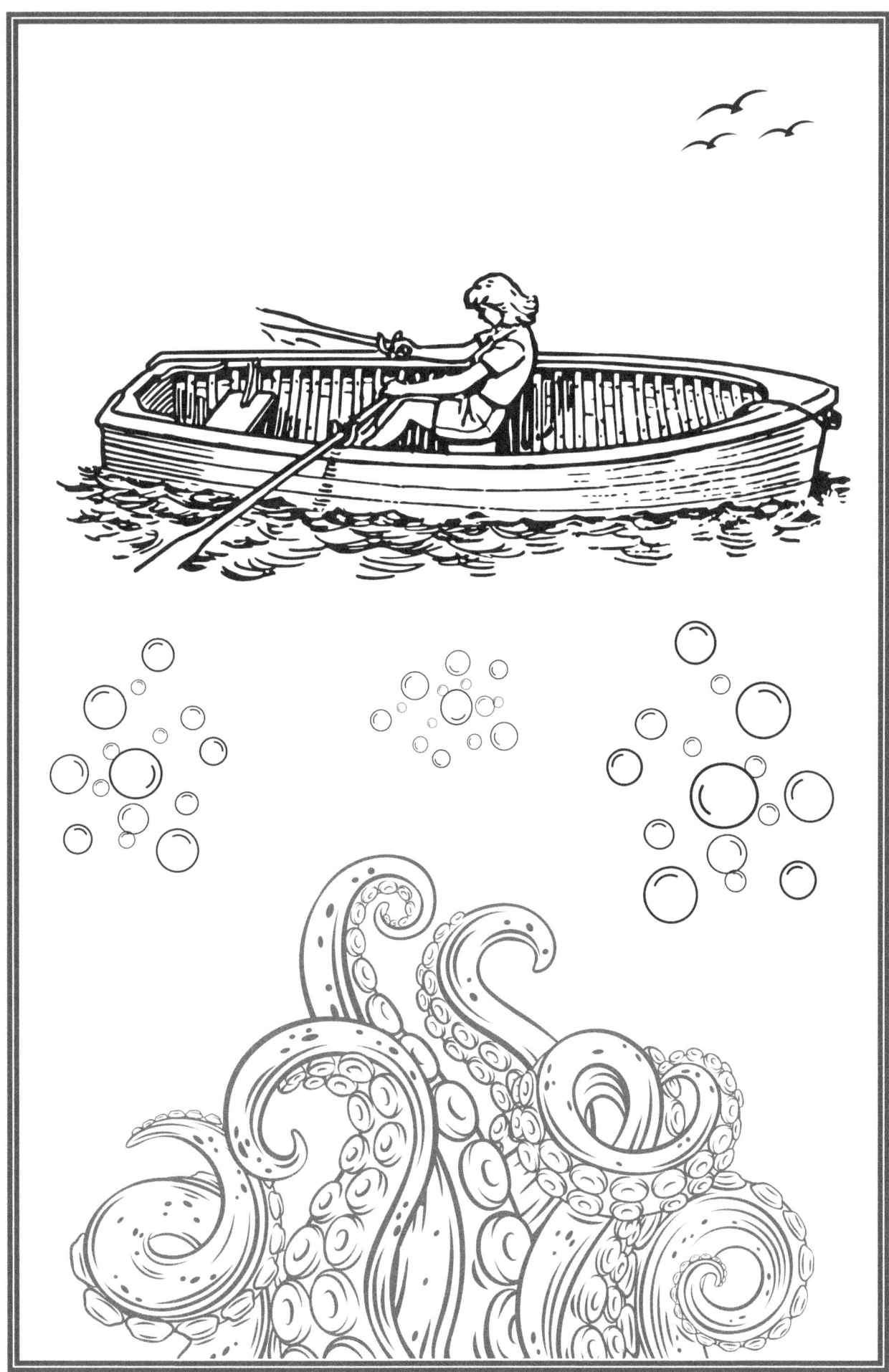

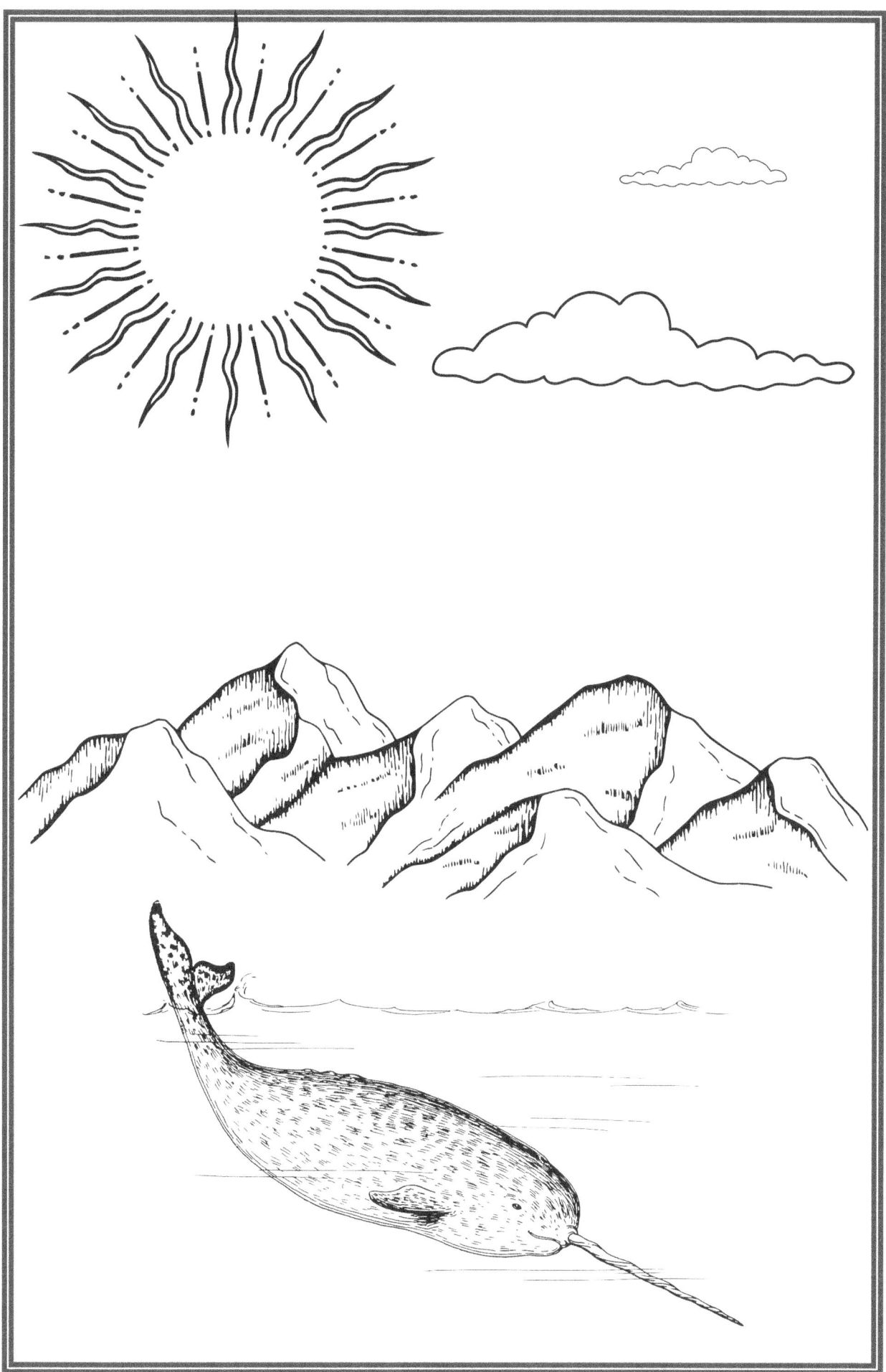

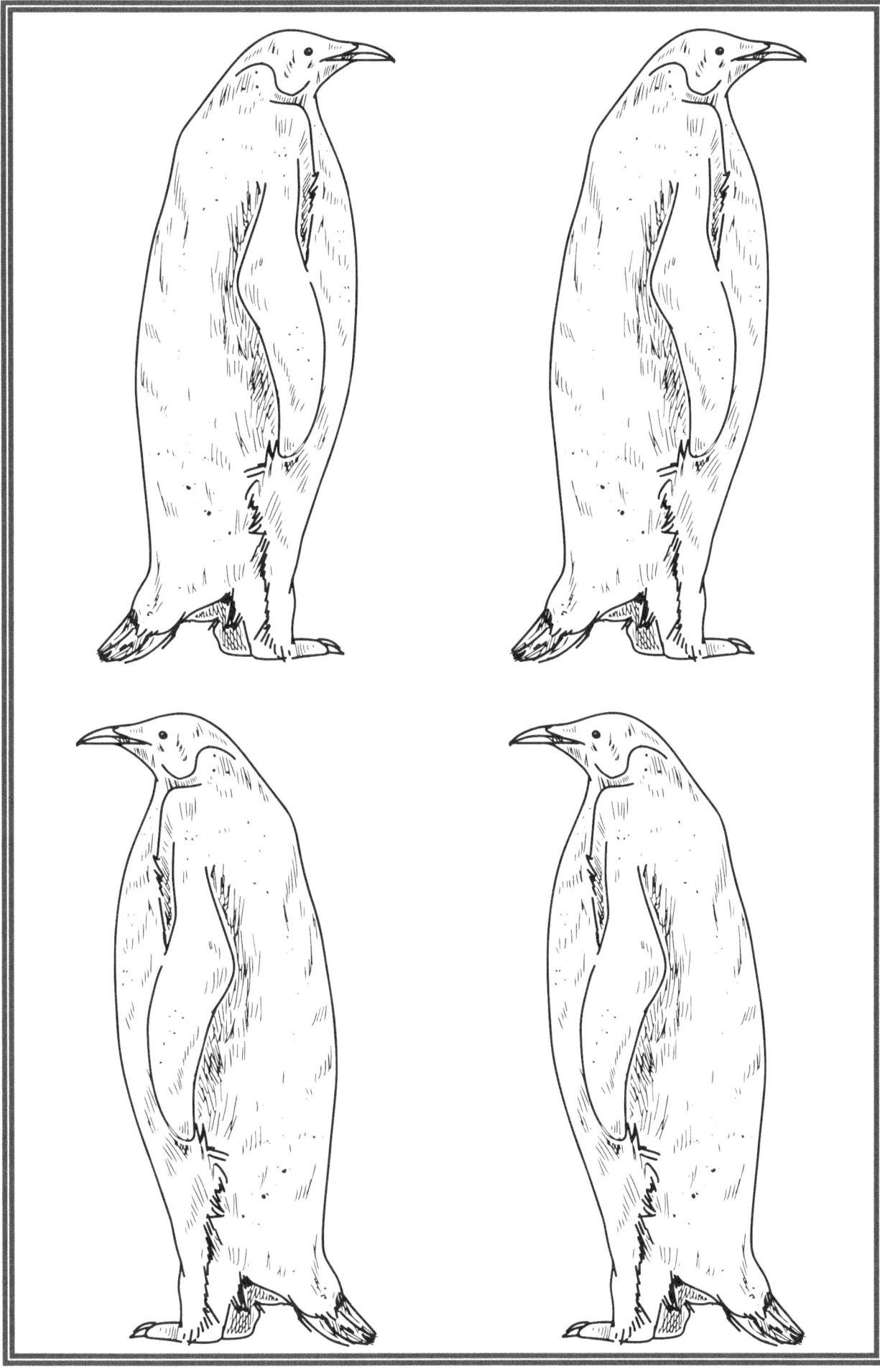

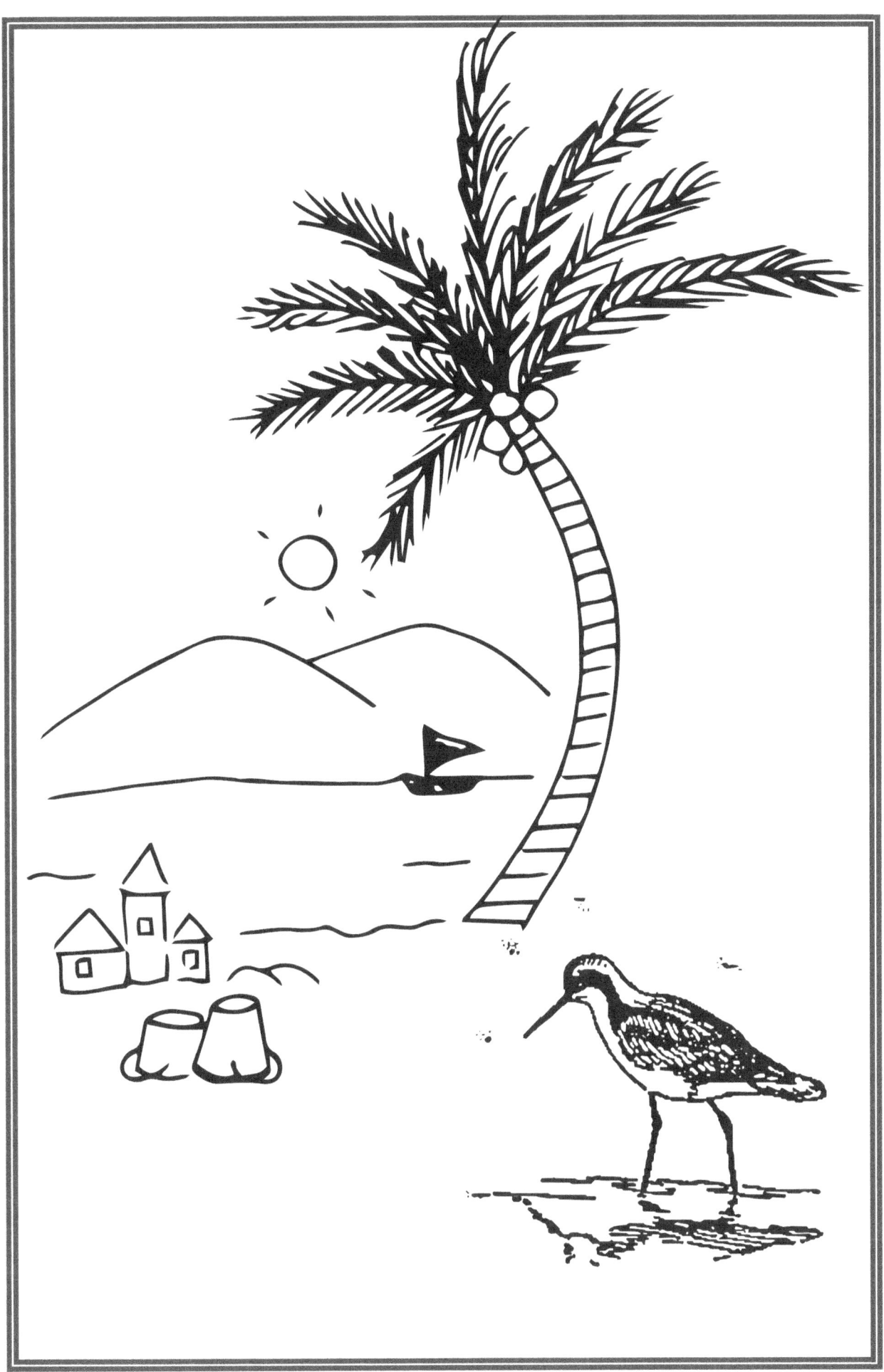

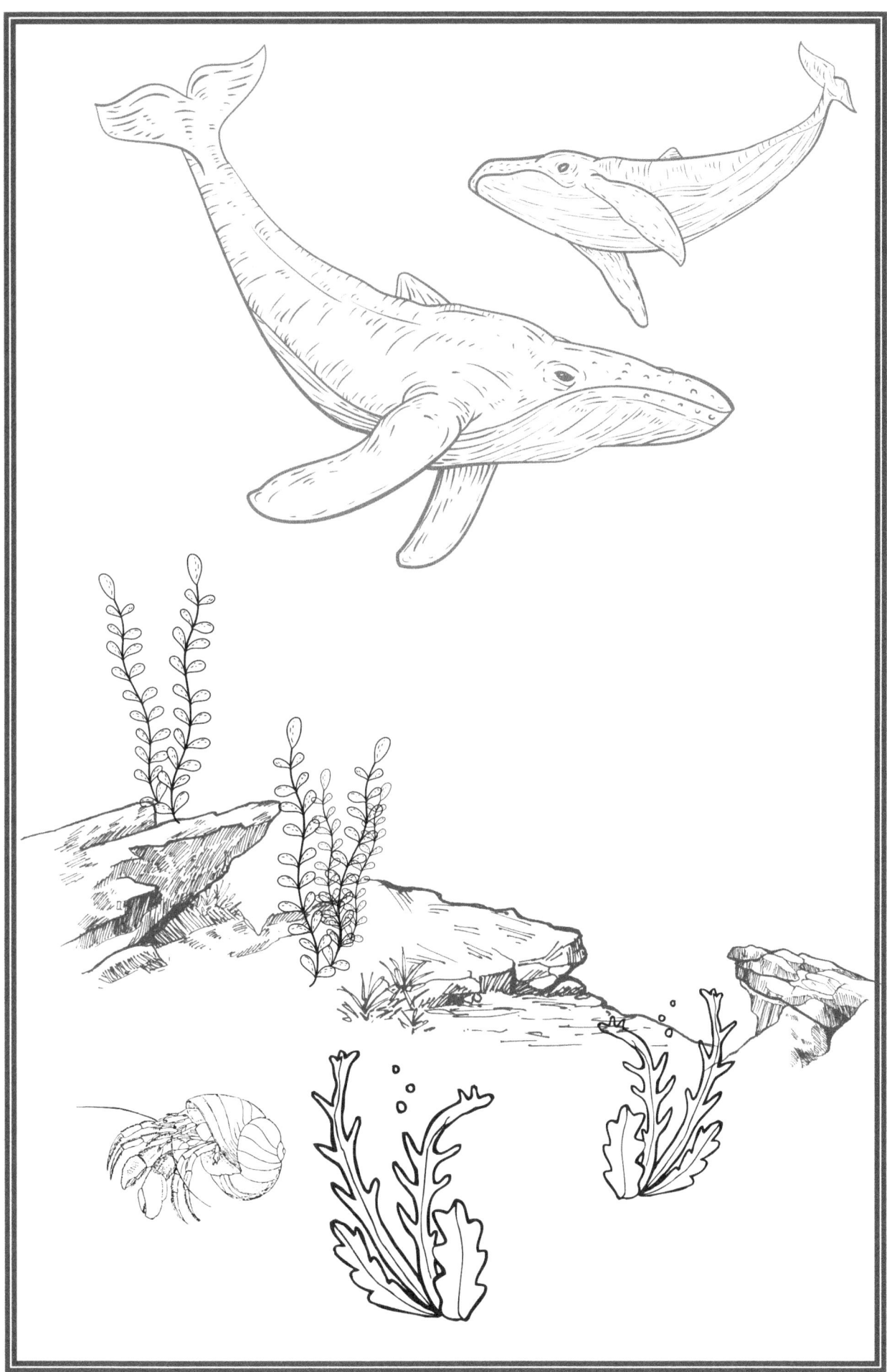

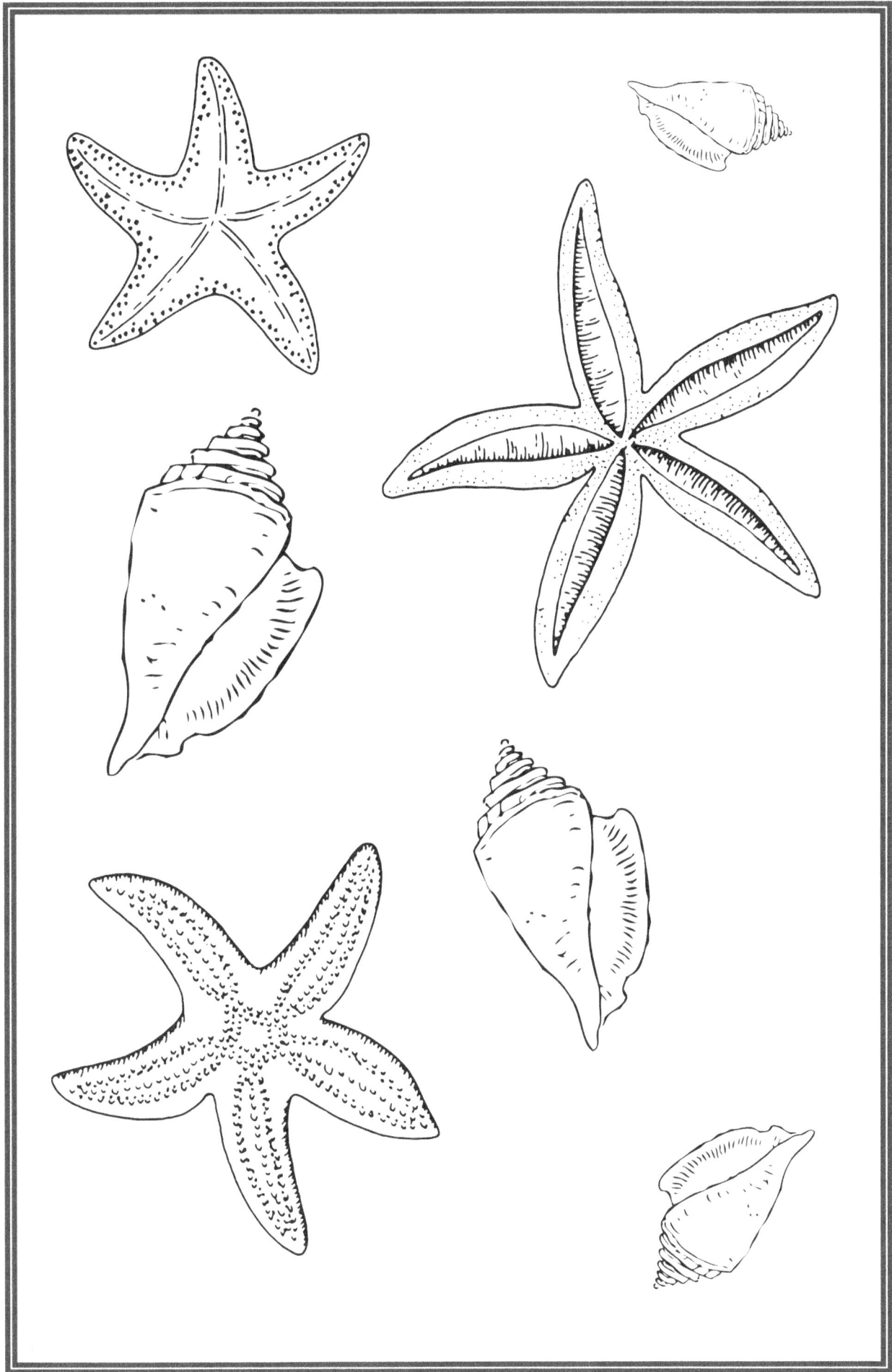

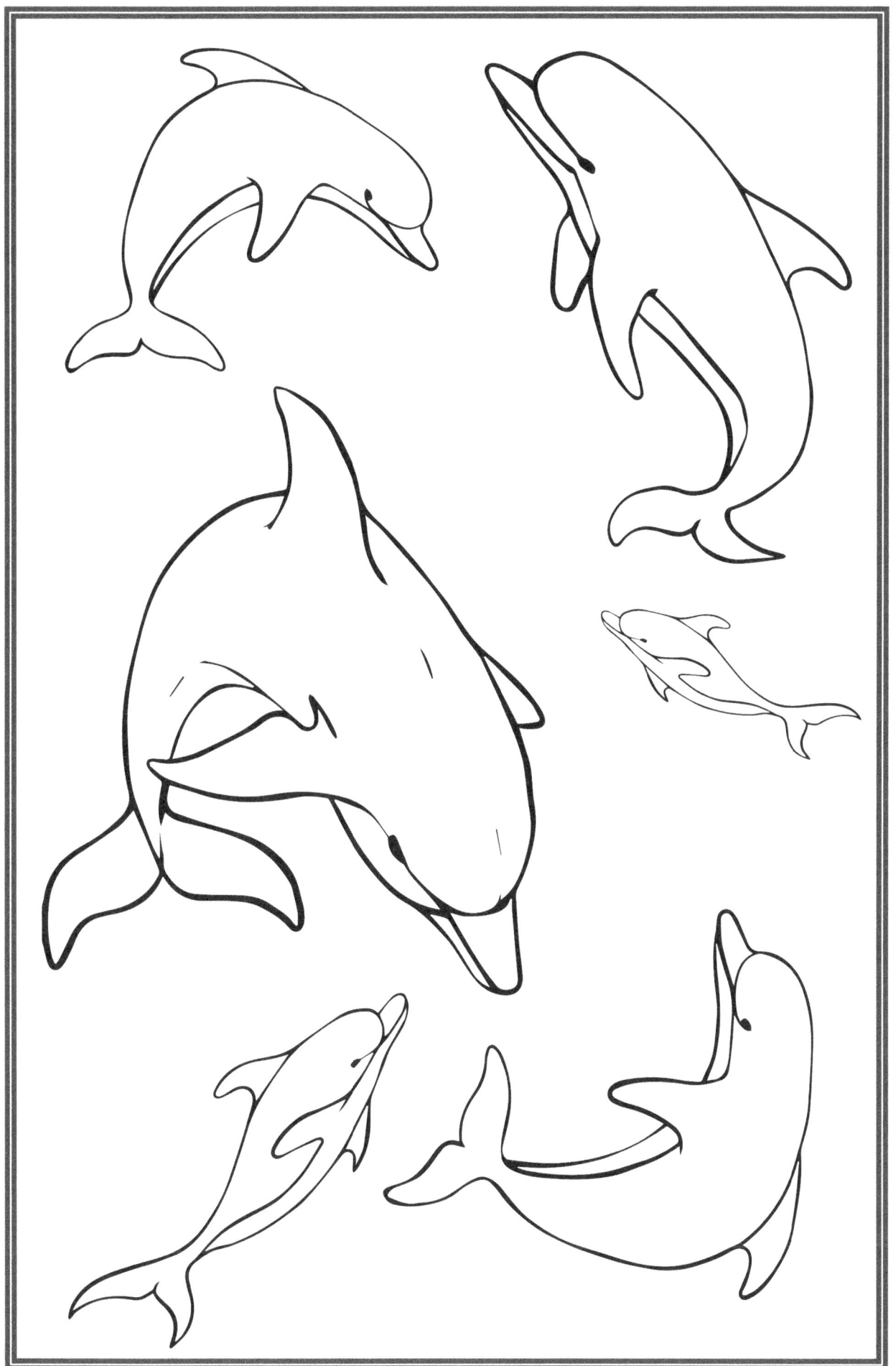

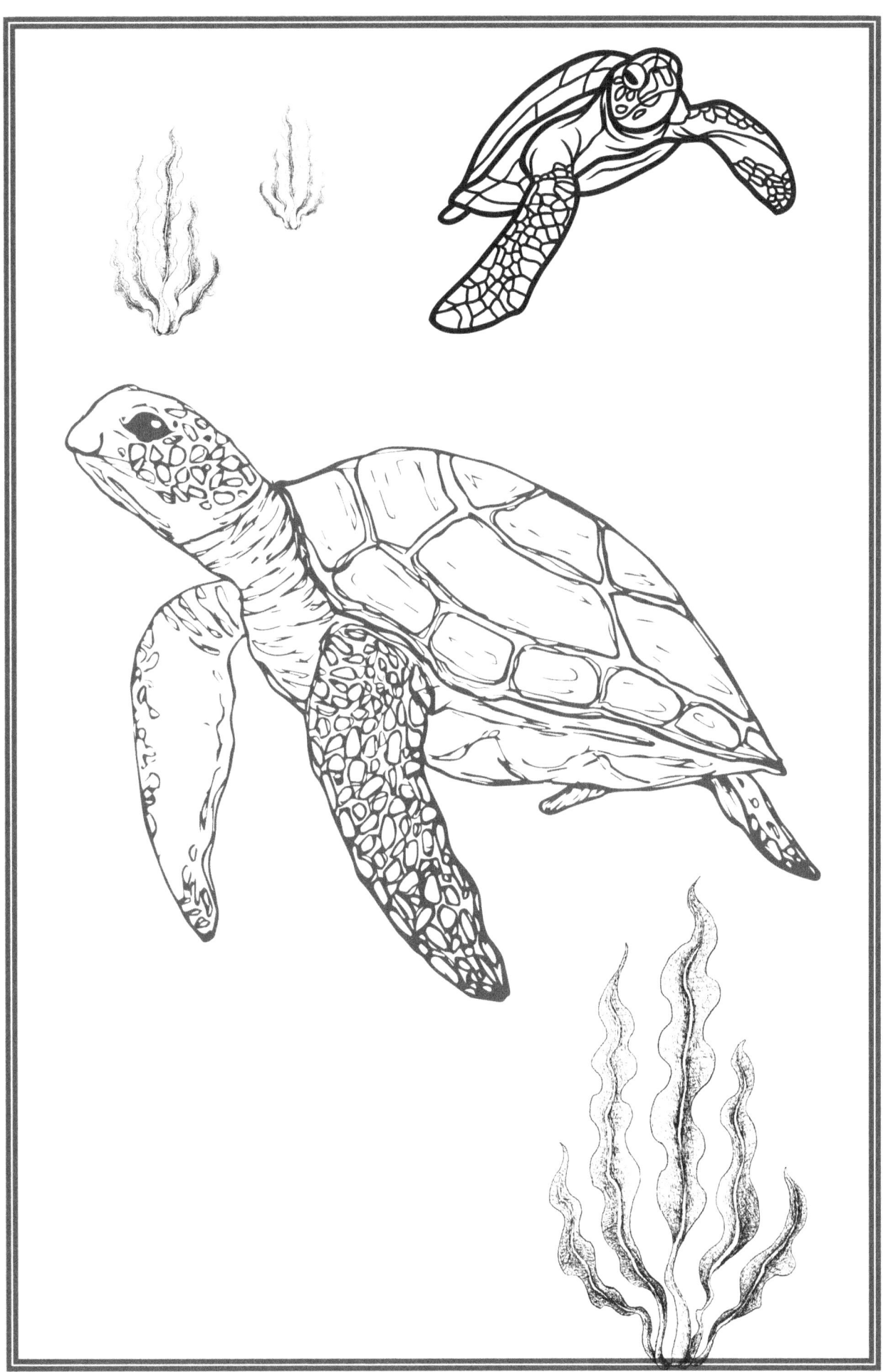

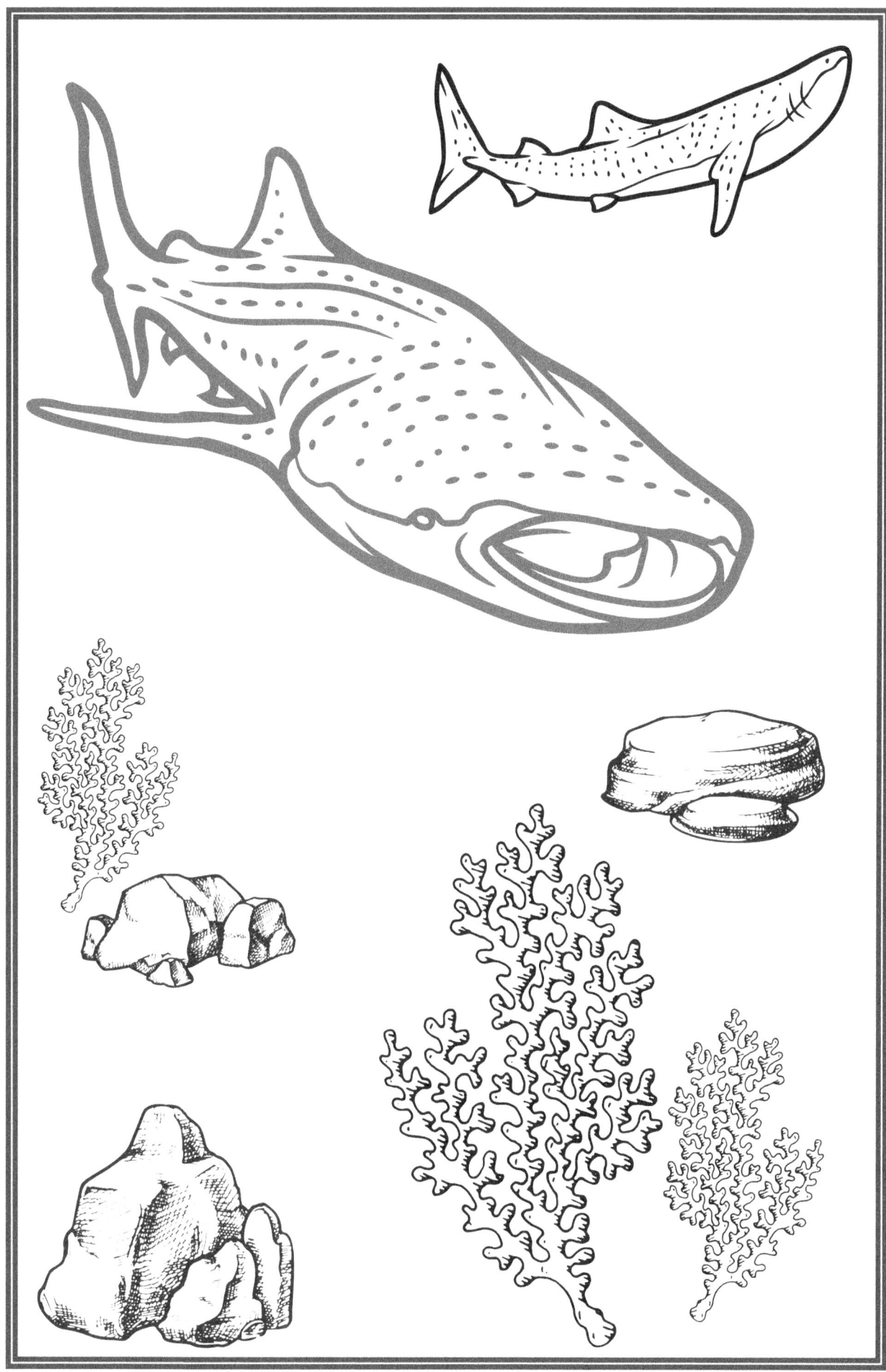

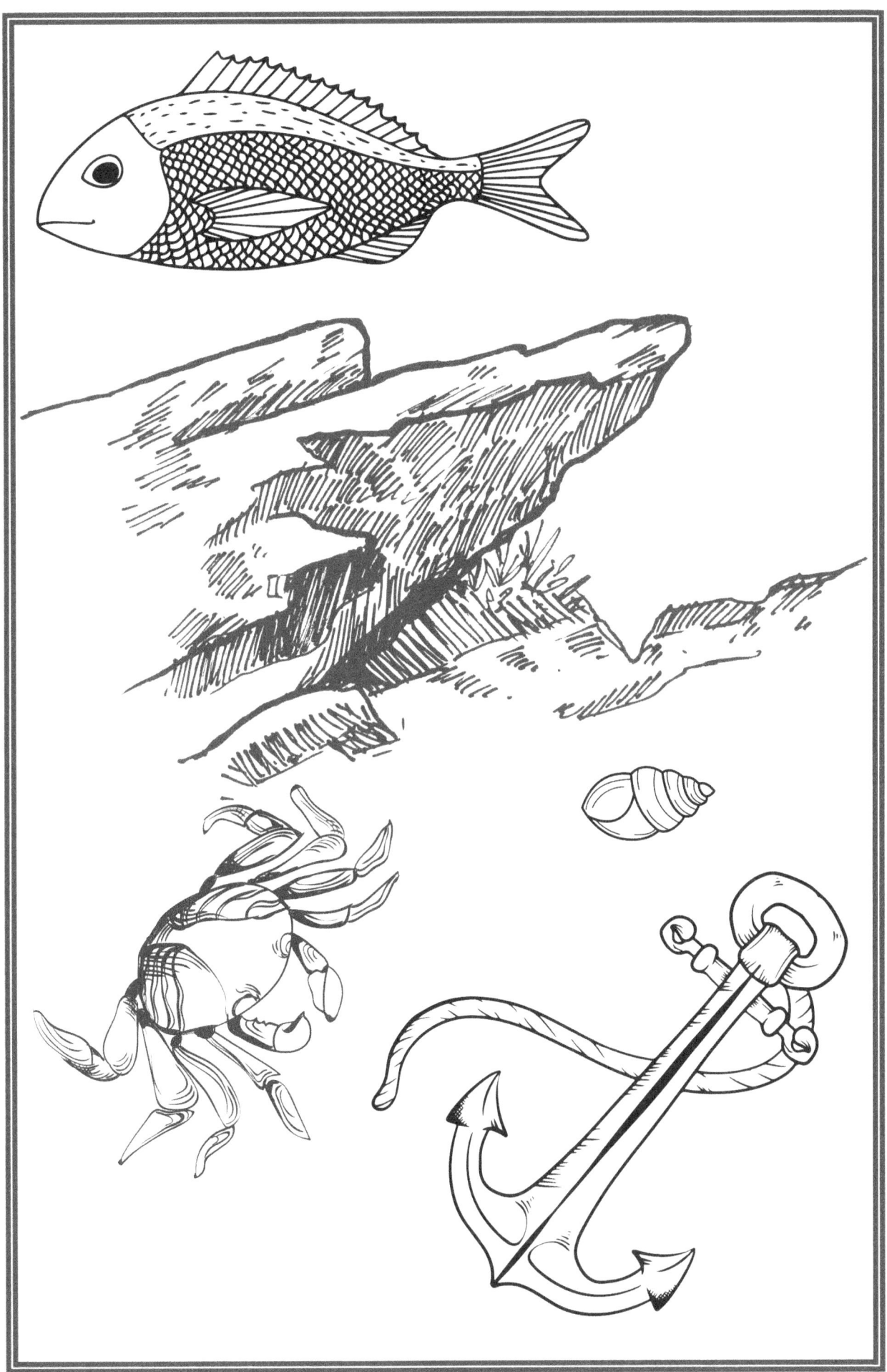

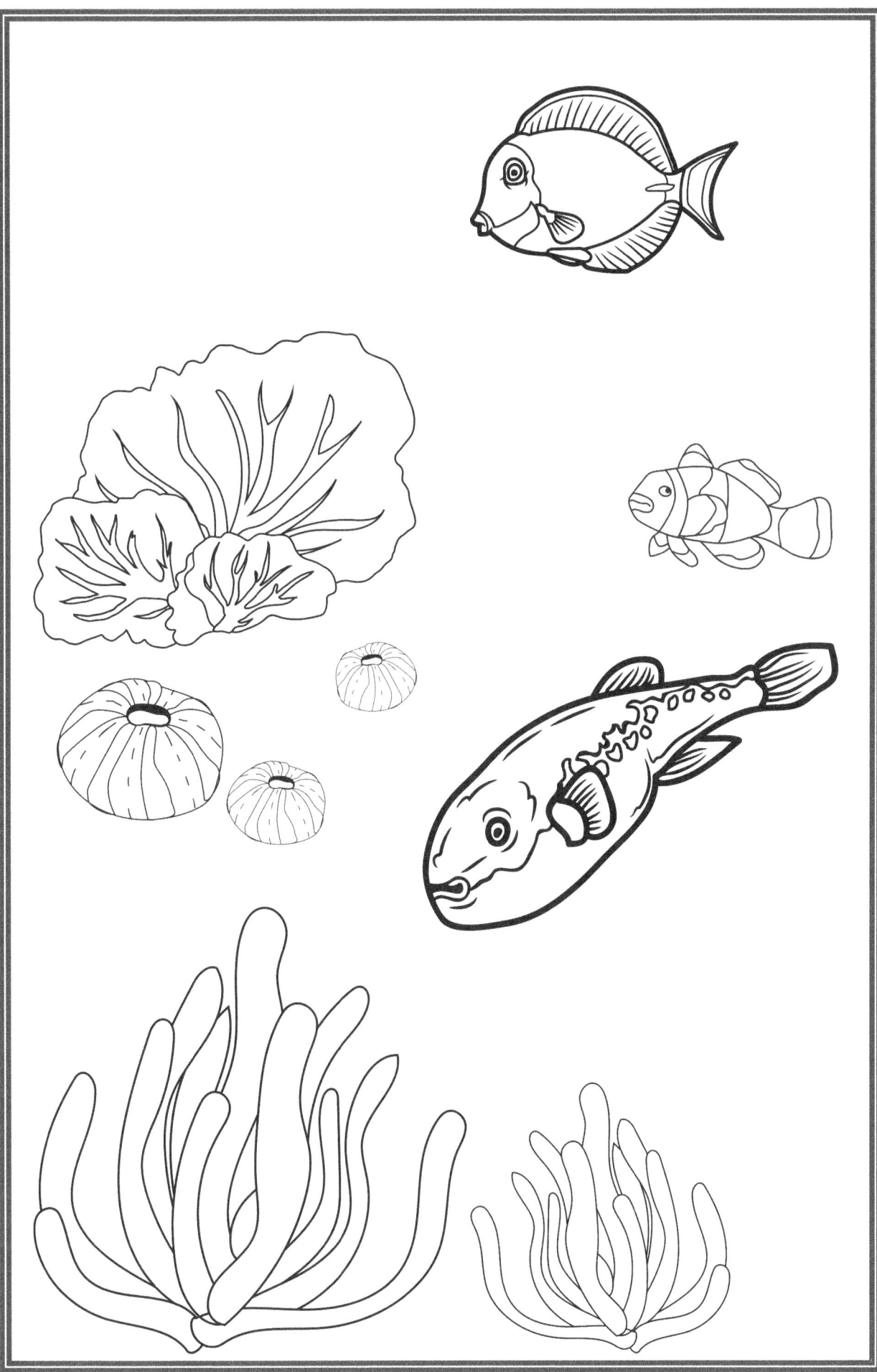

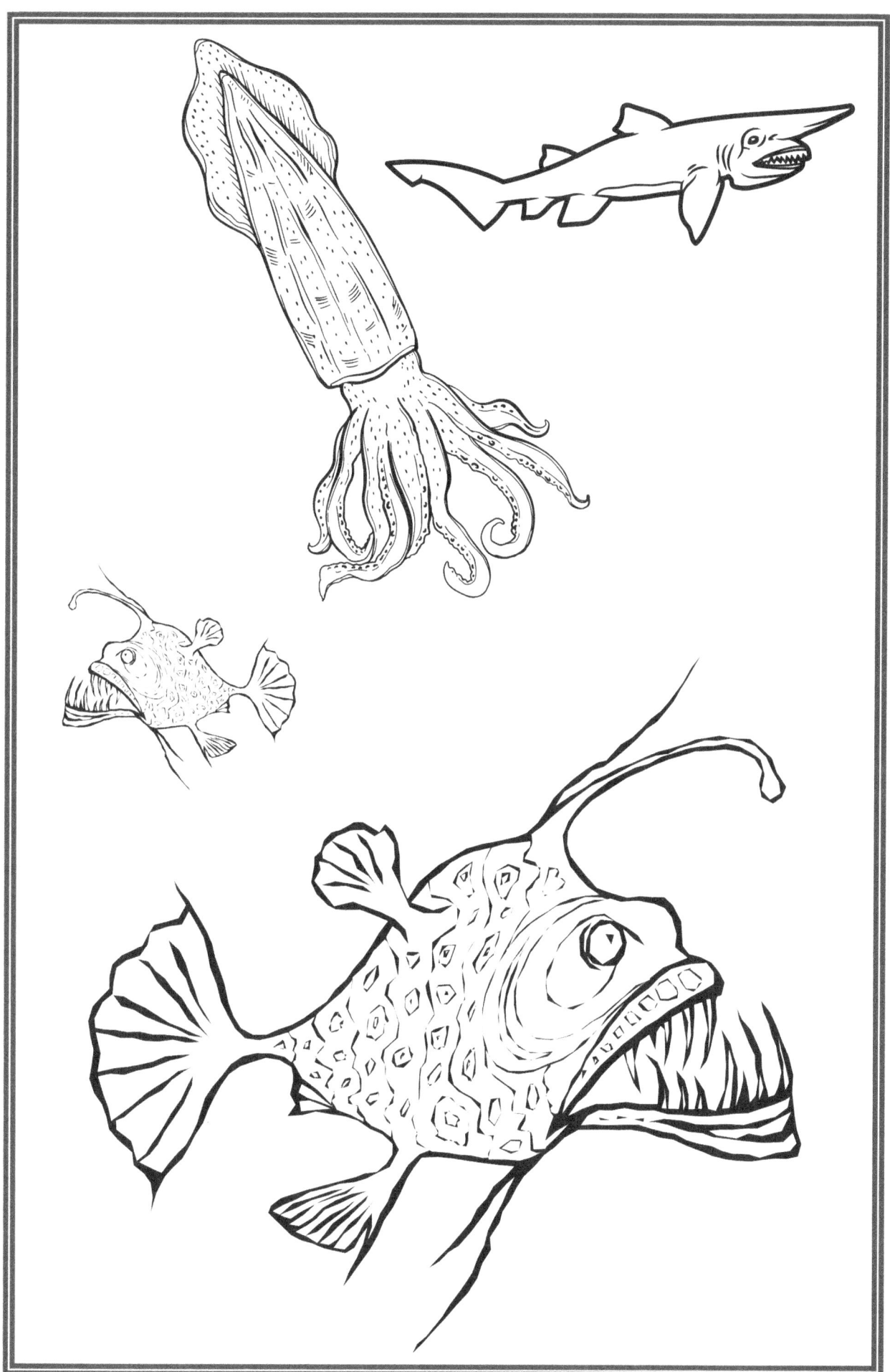

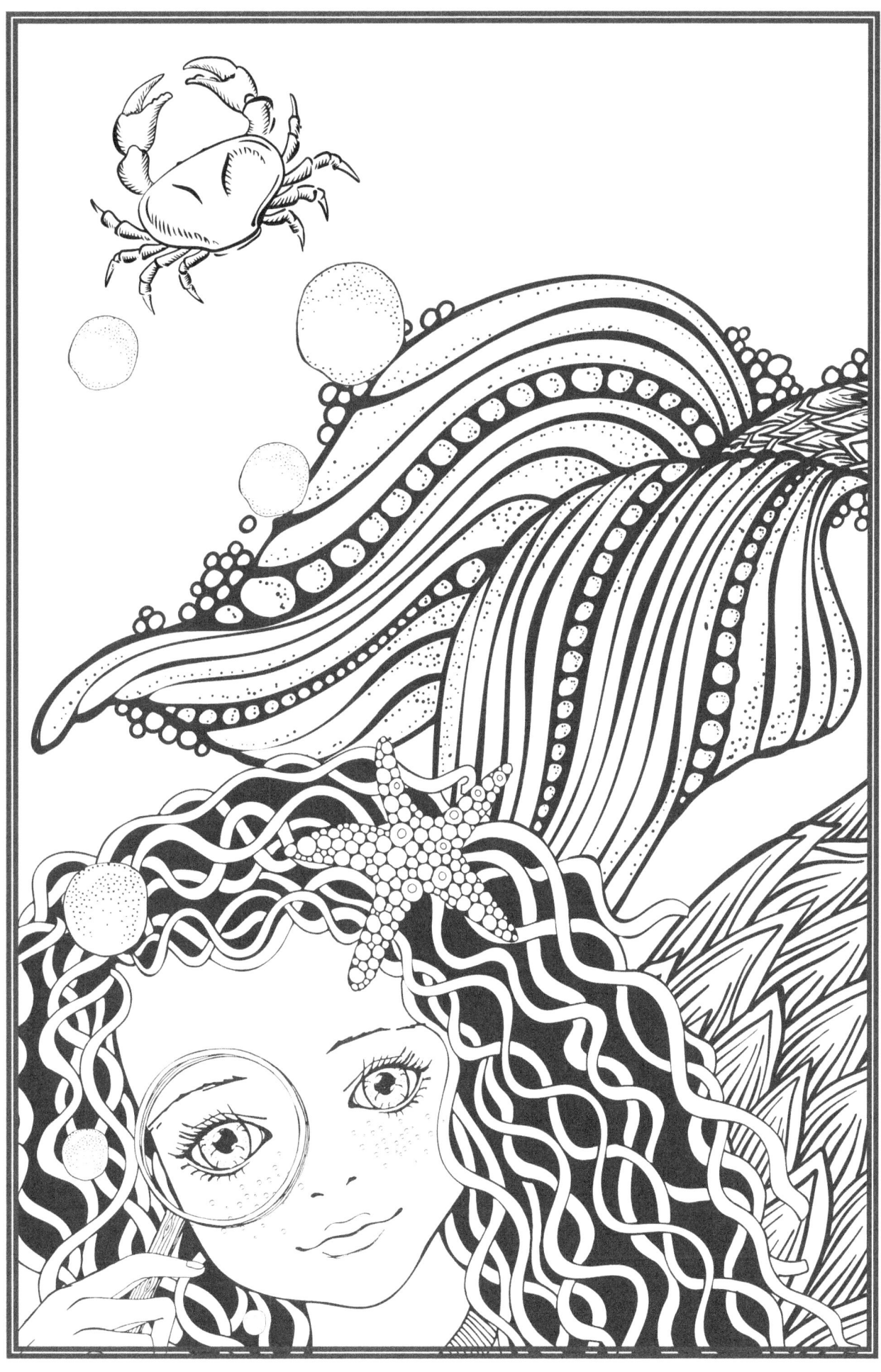

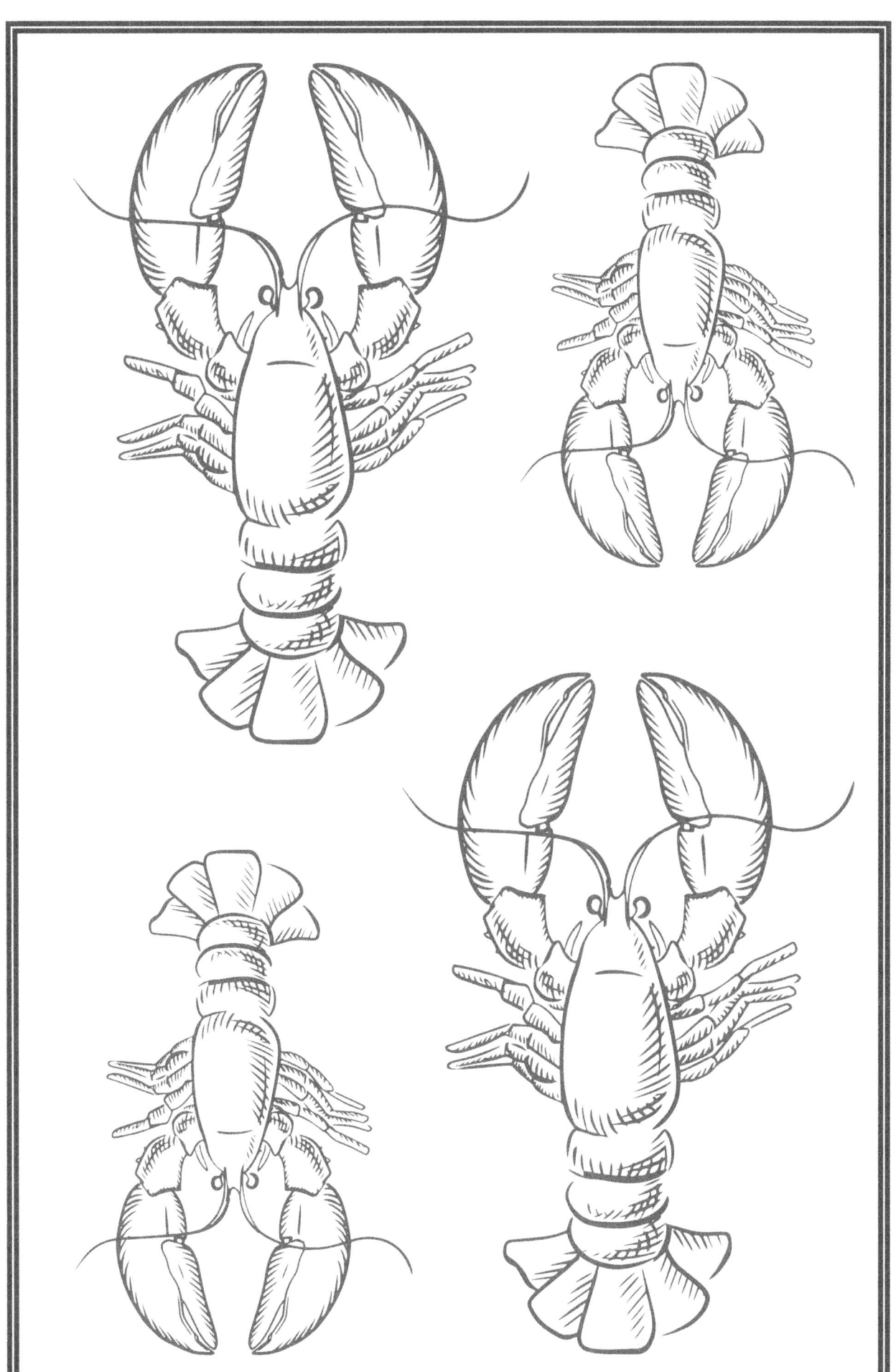

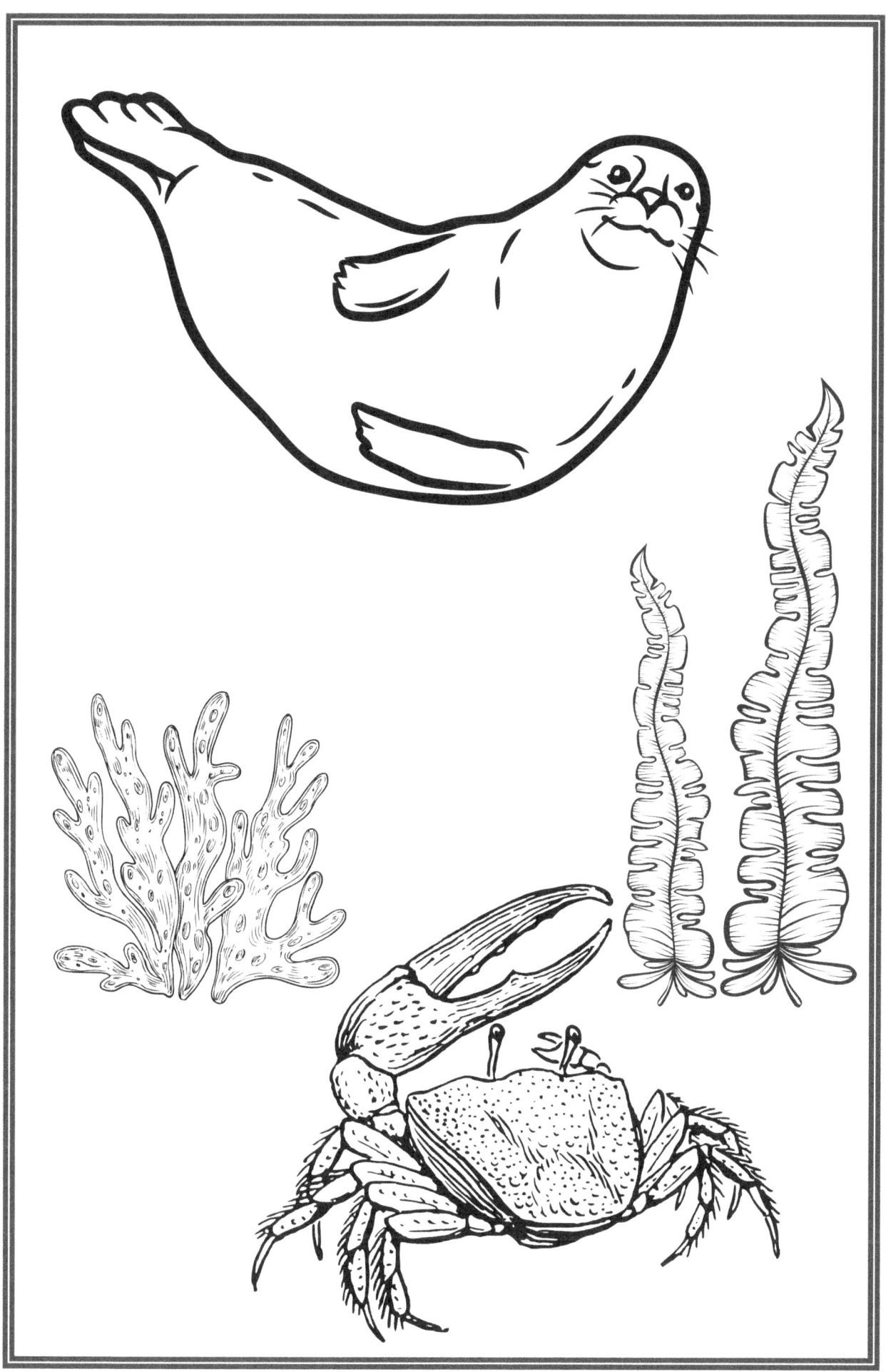

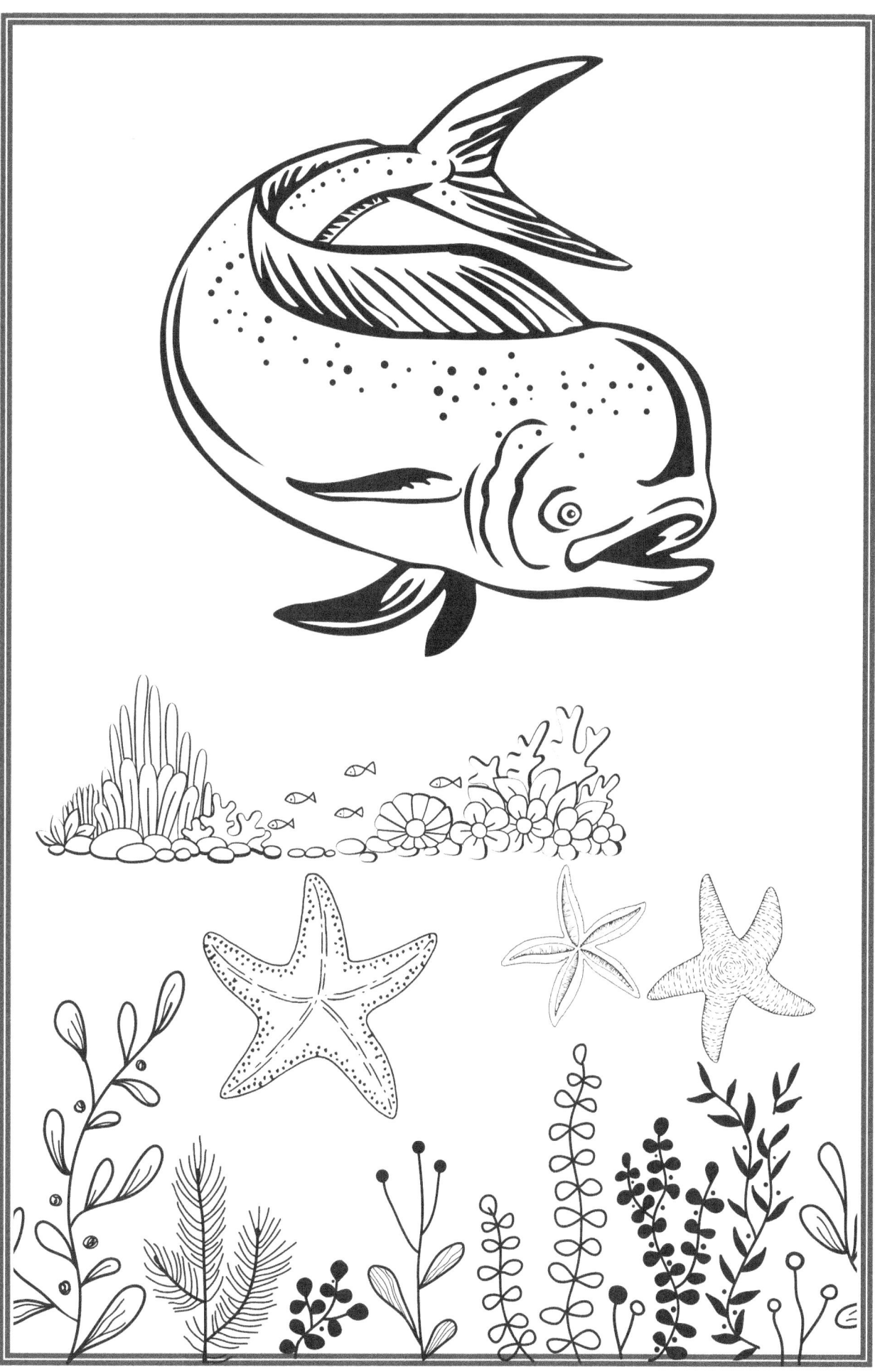

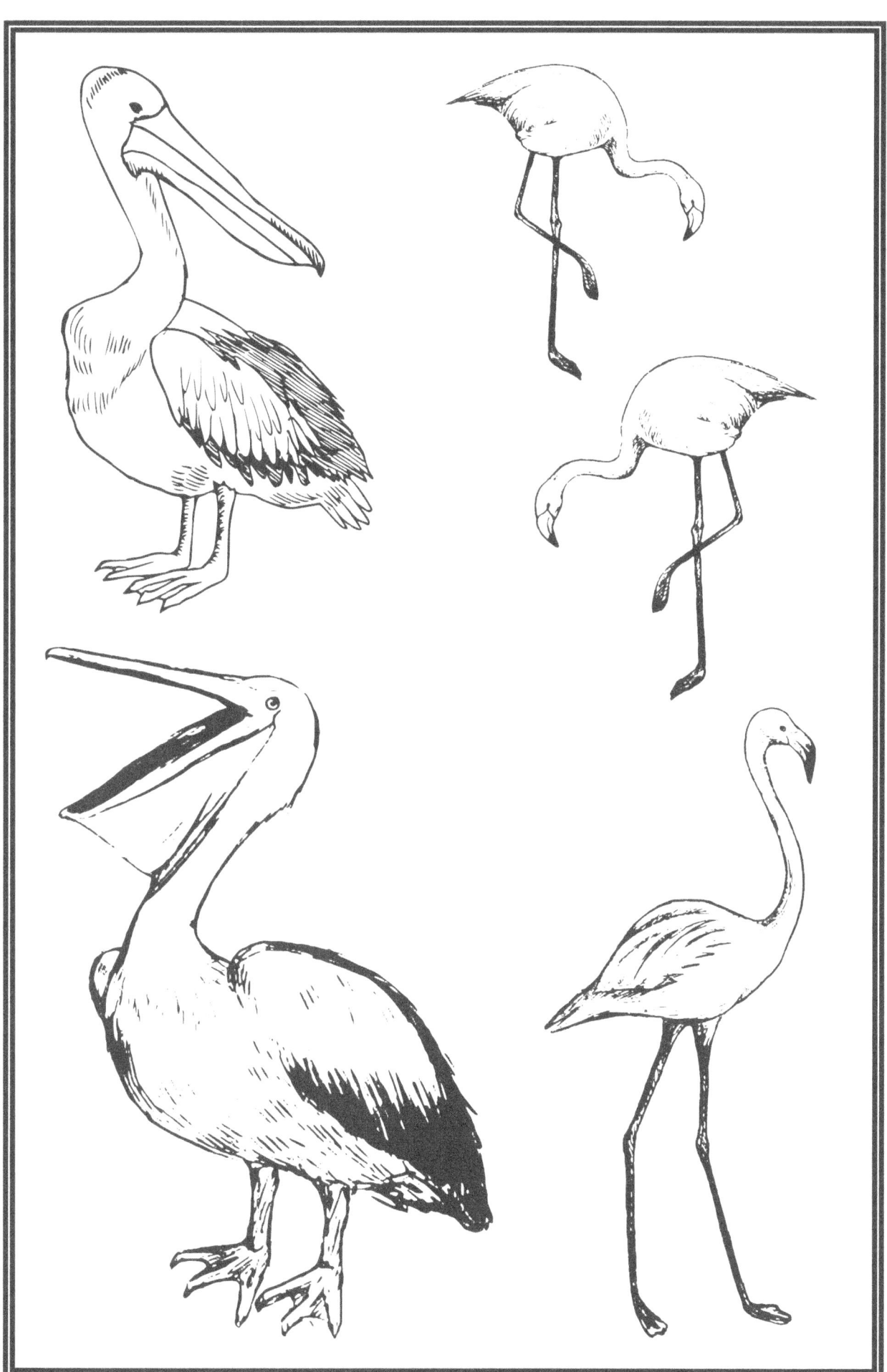

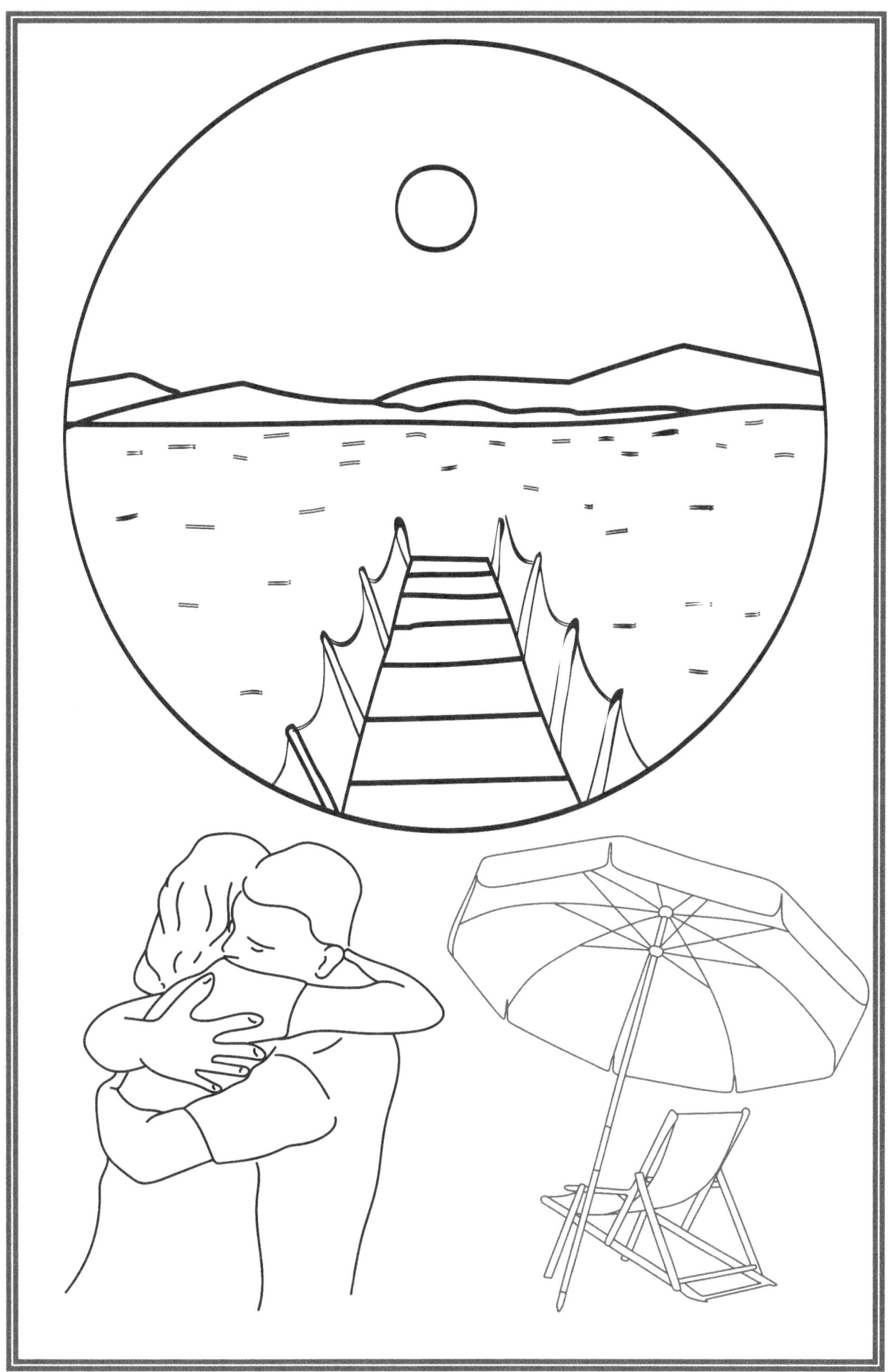

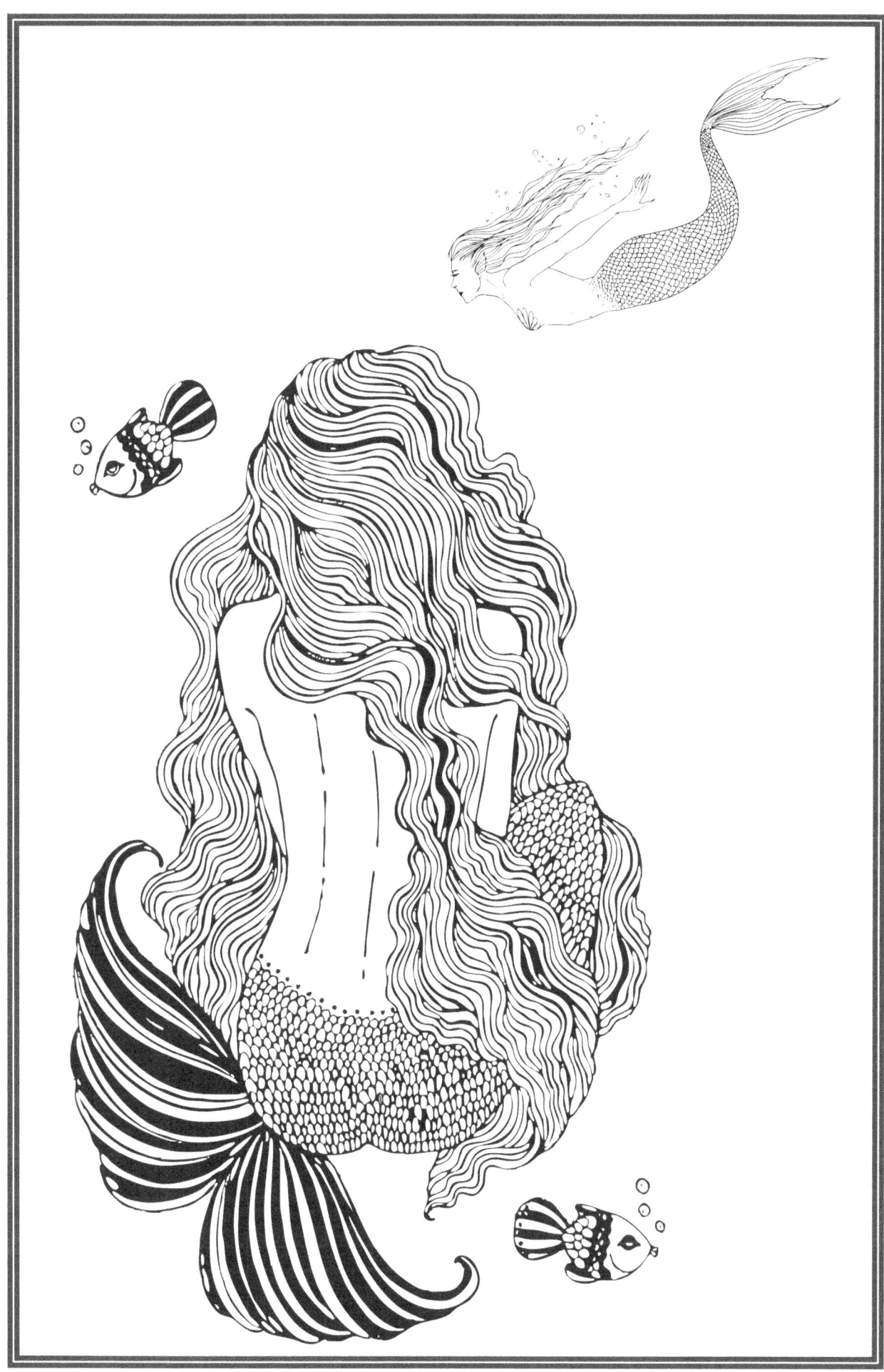

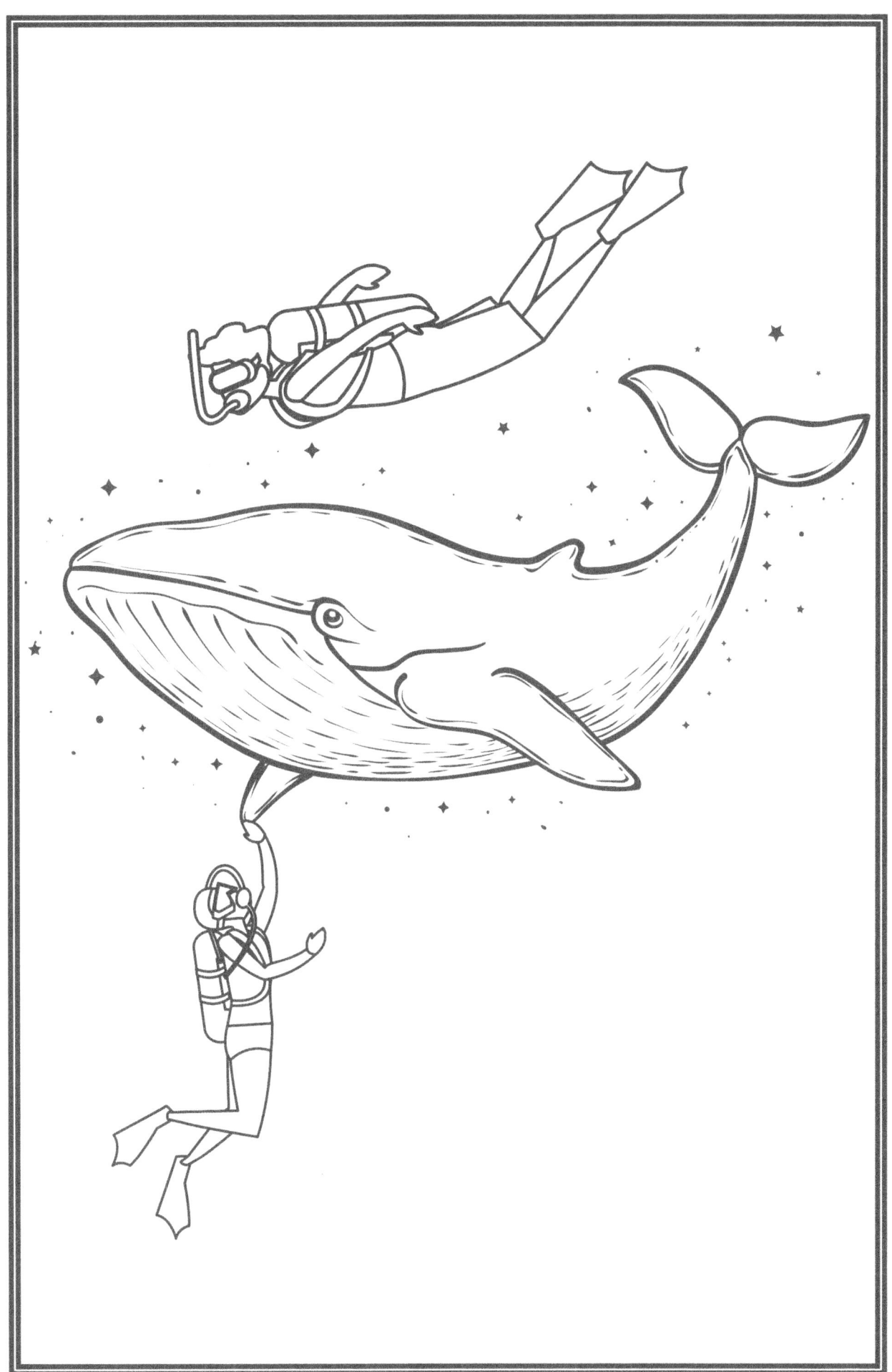

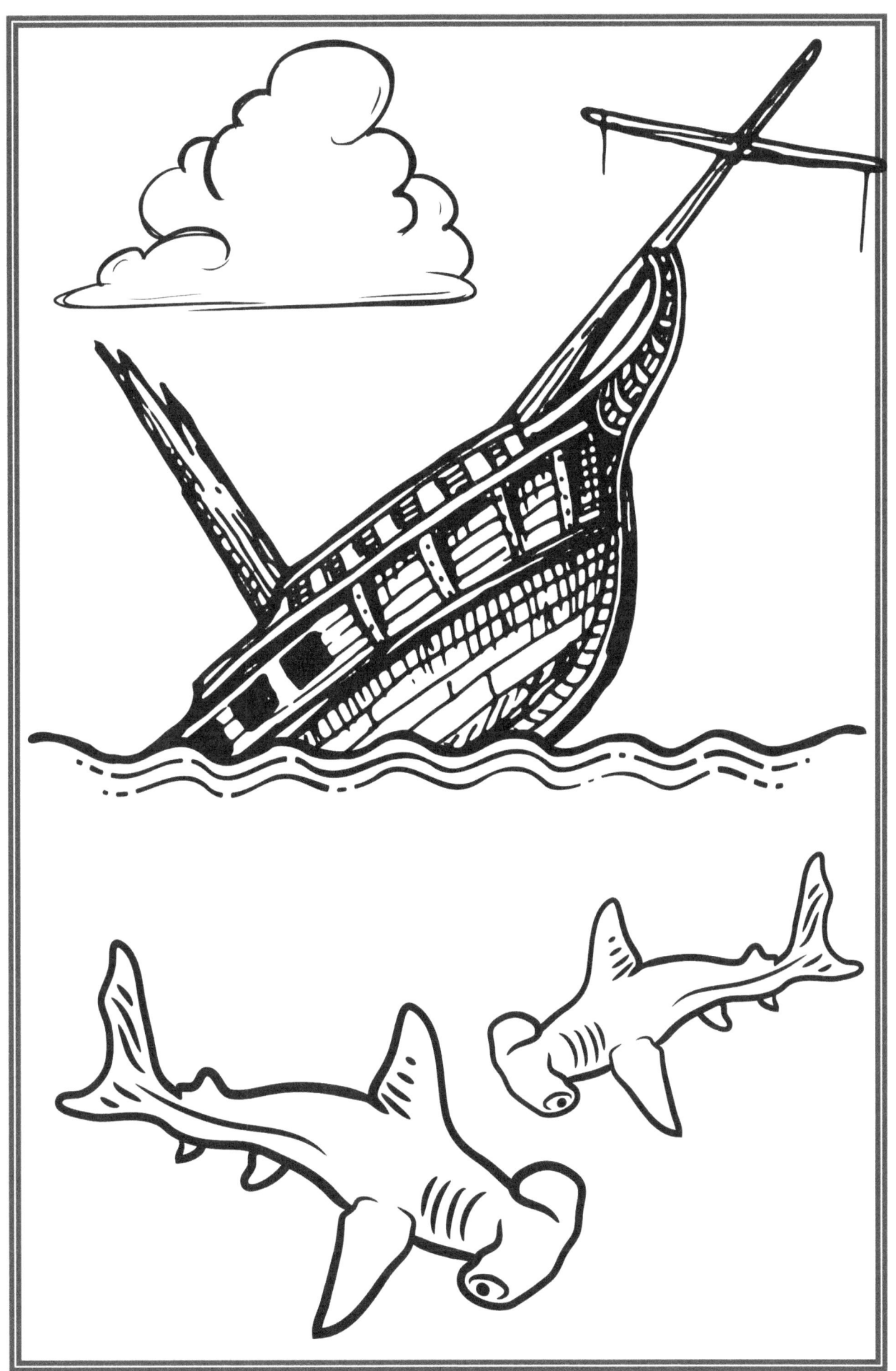

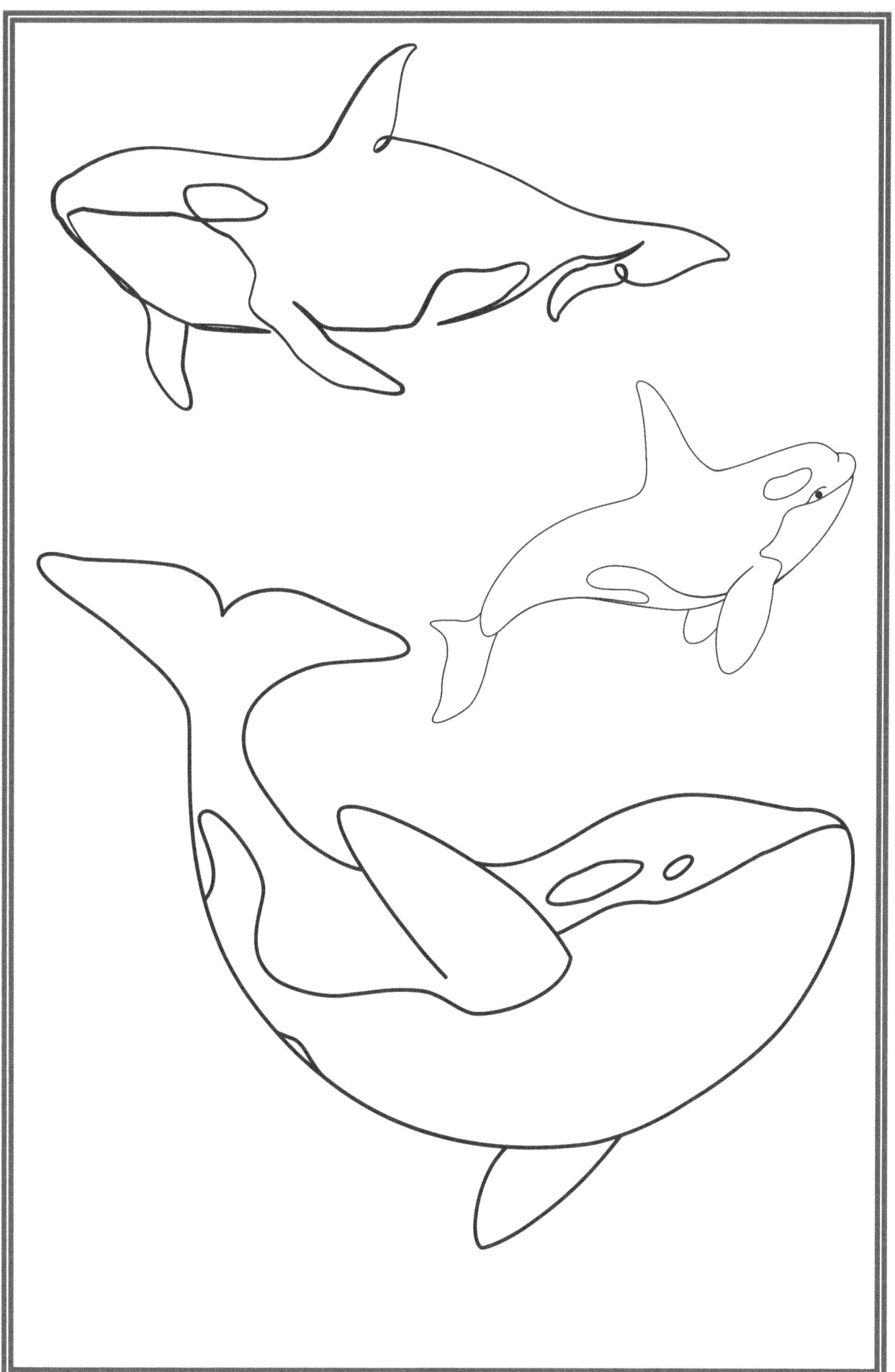

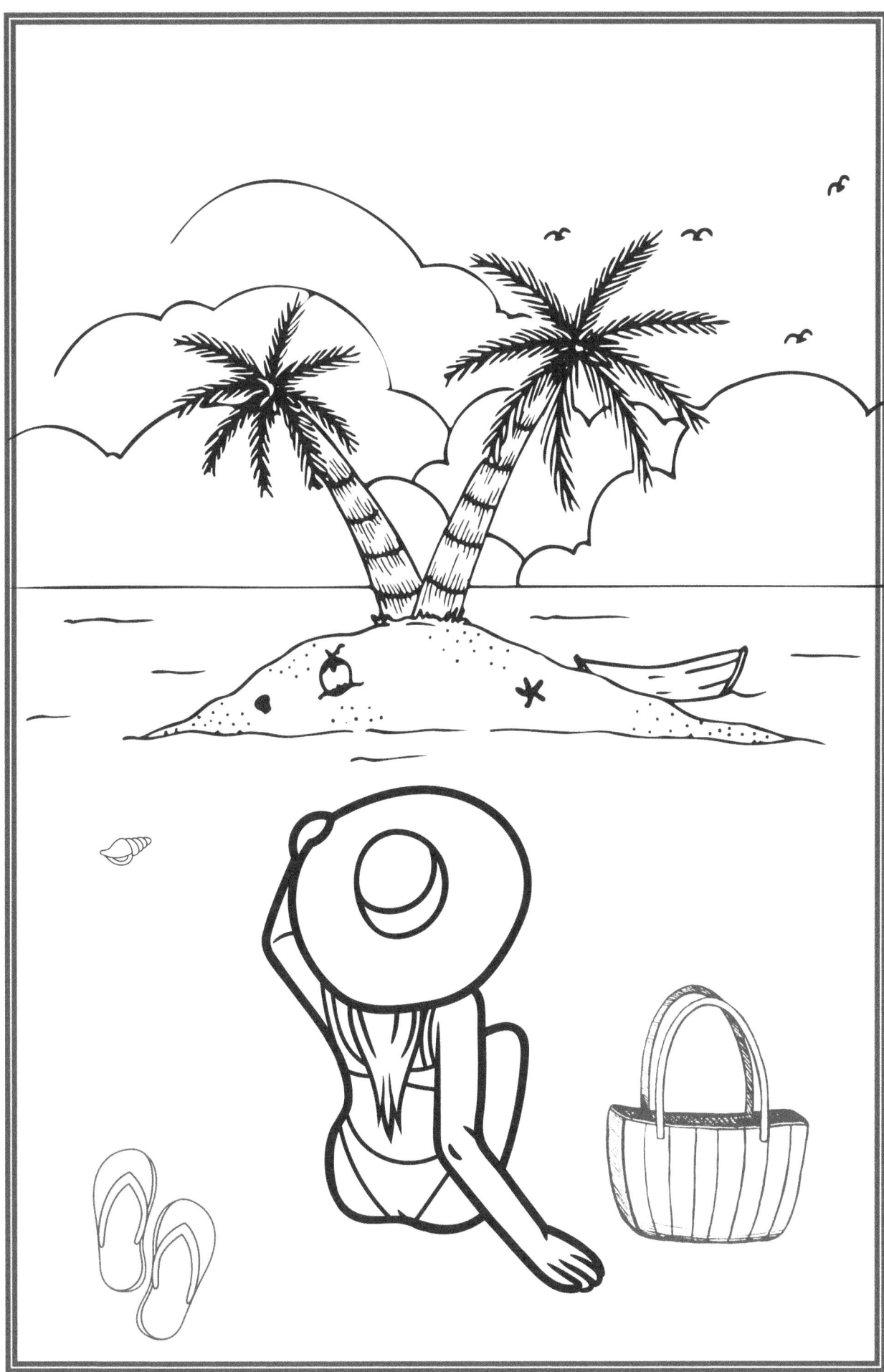

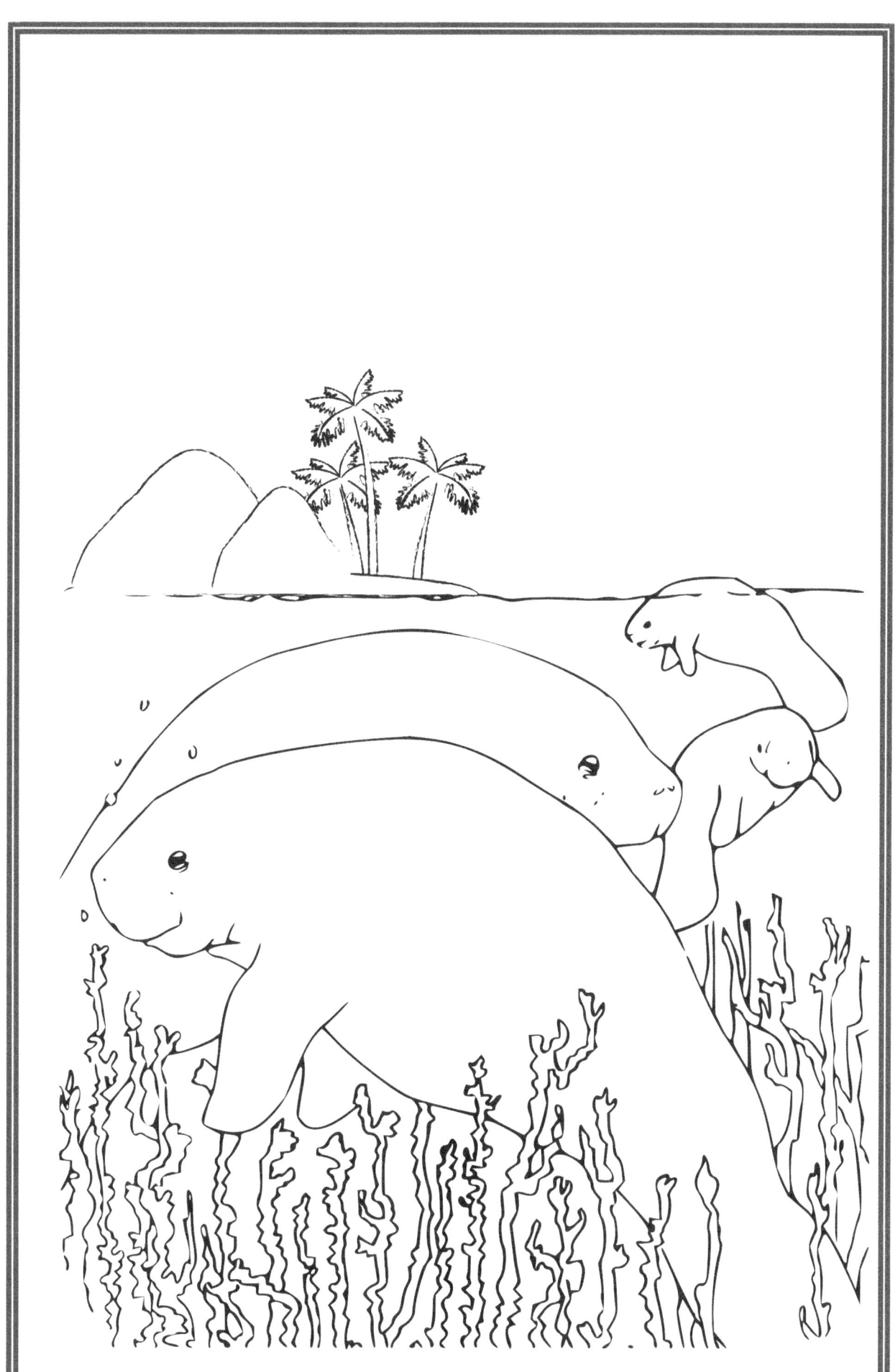

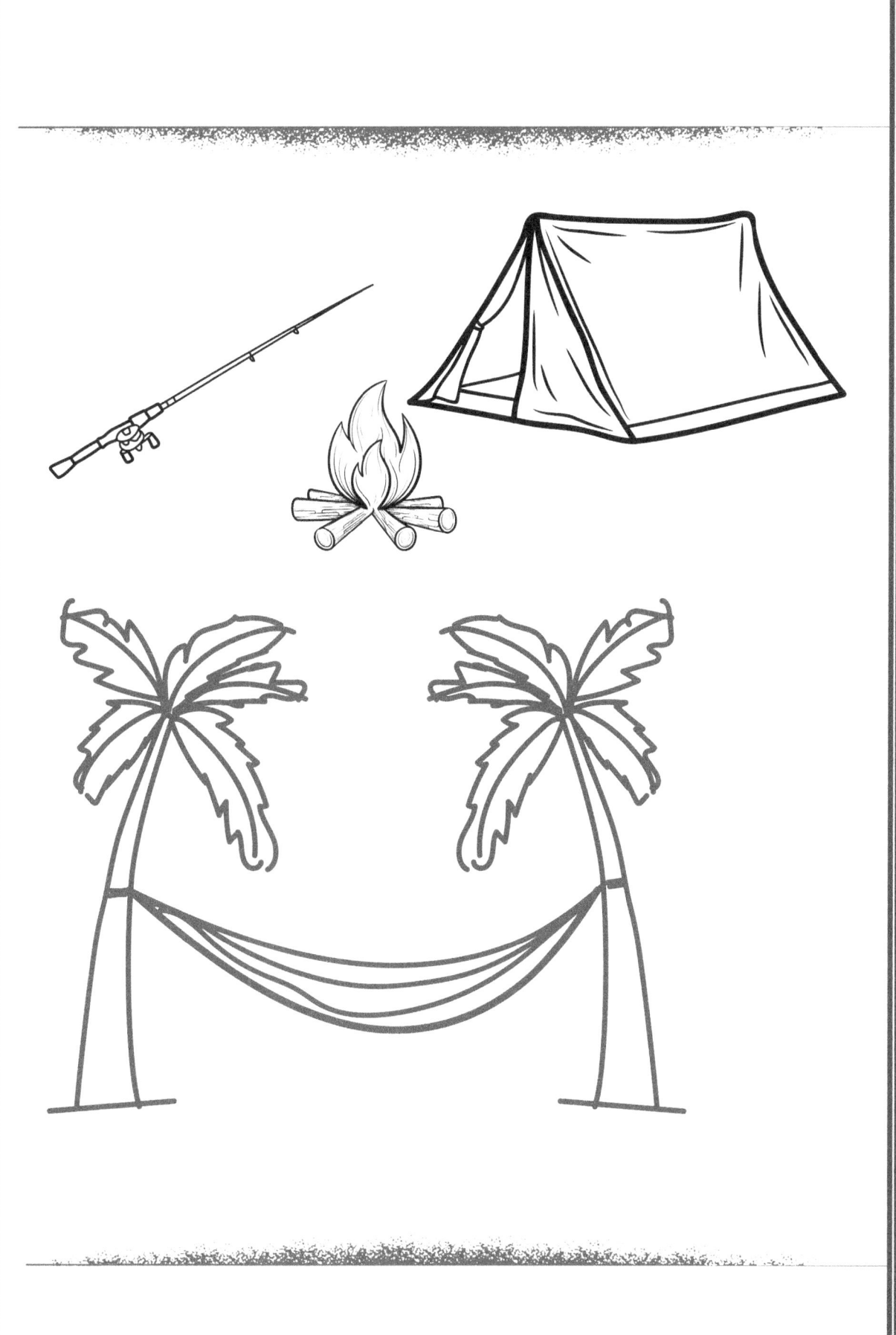

You did it!

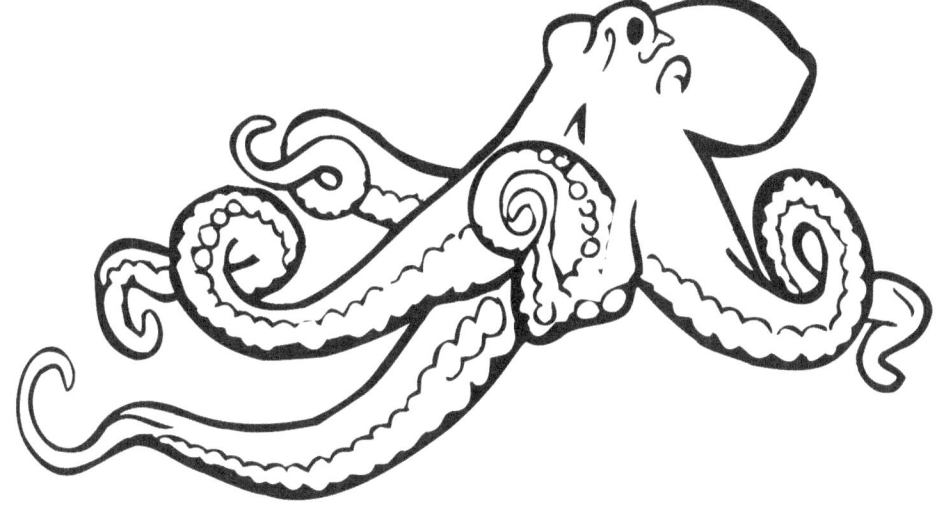

Join our online community & share
your work for a chance to be featured!

@highvibe_earth

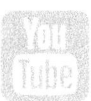  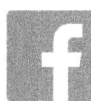

Other books in this series:

Relax & Color Jungles
Relax & Color Forests
Relax & Color Lakes
Relax & Color Cities
Relax & Color Birds
Relax & Color Africa
Relax & Color Quotes

www.highvibe.shop